LIES MY MUSIC TEACHER TOLD ME

Music Theory For Grownups

Gerald Eskelin, D.M.E.

Stage 3 Publishing
Woodland Hills, California

LIES MY MUSIC TEACHER TOLD ME

By Gerald Eskelin, D.M.E

Published by: Stage 3 Publishing
                 5759 Wallis Lane
                 Woodland Hills CA 91367 U.S.A

Manufactured in the United States of America

Copyright 1994 by Gerald R. Eskelin
First Printing 1994
Second Printing 1997
Third Printing 1998
Fourth Printing 1999

Library of Congress Catalog Card Number: 94-68811
ISBN 1-886209-11-1: $14.95 Softcover

Dedicated to all those who studied
music just long enough to be
thoroughly confused.

ABOUT THE AUTHOR

Gerald Eskelin has been making music for more than four decades. His vocal group, the L.A. Jazz Choir, has twice been nominated for a Grammy award. Having also been a college professor of music for thirty years, including tenures at the University of Southern California, California Institute of the Arts and Pierce College in Los Angeles, he has had considerable experience in both commercial and academic music. His conducting experience includes almost everything from symphony orchestra to marching band and master chorale to pop choir. He has sung opera, show music, jazz, barbershop and even a bit of southern gospel.

His expertise on musical matters is frequently called on by the Los Angeles legal community. He has testified in court on behalf of such well-known personalities as John Fogerty, Stevie Wonder, "Roger Rabbit," Michael Jackson, and The Isley Brothers, and has given musicological opinions for a great many others, including Tom Petty, Ray Parker Jr., and Madonna.

His academic credits include a Doctor of Music Education and Master of Arts degrees from Indiana University and a Bachelor of Arts degree from Florida Southern College.

ACKNOWLEDGMENTS

This project was born about a decade ago when the planning committee for a MACCC convention (that's Music Association of California Community Colleges) was discussing ideas for the theory session. After a number of old tired topics were considered at some length, I tossed out the possible topic "Lies My Music Teacher Told Me." After the chuckles subsided, all eyes turned toward me. Monty, the chairman, said, "Sounds good, Jer. You're on."

So this gave me a chance to bounce some ideas off my colleagues in a setting where they were somewhat obligated to pay attention. The session seemed to go well and generated some lively conversation. Two years later, when I was no longer on the board, Monty called and asked me to repeat the "lies lecture" for those who missed it the first time. I assumed he wasn't able to get anyone else and knew I would be an easy mark. I was told later that it was the only time in the group's history that a specific lecture had been called back by popular demand. Whether or not that was true, it did suggest that some of my out-of-step ideas seemed to get a positive response from those who are supposed to know better.

So, with the encouragement of Monty LaBonte, a valued friend and probably the most influential member MACCC ever had, I decided to write this book. Monty died last March. Not only will we miss him very much, but I am personally disappointed that he left before I could present him with a copy of the product that grew from his inspiration.

During the years following the lectures, I began to put the "lies" down on paper and a great many of my students, colleagues and singers were kind enough to look over my pages and offer comments. There were so many that I am not going to start naming. I'm sure to forget someone who shouldn't be forgotten.

However, the two readers who were most influential in shaping the manuscript into its present form are Stephanie Vitali, lovely wife of one of my singers who just happened to be an editor, and Stephen Piazza, my very musical department chairperson at Pierce College. Both Stephanie and Steve con-vinced me to get rid of the swear words in order to sell books in the midwest.

Most importantly, my very talented and beautiful wife Marlene worked many hours transforming my yellow-pad scribblings into nice typewritten pages. This was before I bought my Macintosh and resurrected my junior-high typing skills. This development got her promoted to principle provider of inspiration.

My four kids -- Dionne, Todd, Edward and Erik -- are all grown up and out doing their own thing. They had nothing to do with the production of this book, but I thought they might like to see their names in print.

OVERTURE

(Don't skip this part.)

When we were children, our parents and teachers told us things about life and the nature of the world that we absorbed into our "body of truth" with innocent and uncritical faith. And, for the most part, the ideas they instilled in us were pretty good ones. Most of us have a solid concept of "private property" and a healthy respect for the "rights of others" and things like that. Usually we were encouraged to develop a strong faith in something -- God, truth, friendship, ourselves -- or some combination of these.

We were also told some "temporary" truths that would serve us while we were young but could later be discarded or modified when we grew up to be responsible adults. "Don't go into the street" later became "look both ways before you cross the street." When we got a drivers license we were told, "Don't drive faster than the speed limit," which later was modified by the phrase, "unless everyone else is doing it, too." Actually, our parents and teachers didn't really *tell* us about that modification. We learned it by watching them.

Sometimes I wonder whether they had any doubts about the things they taught us. When my parents said to "always tell the truth," I know they wanted me to do that. However, they also wanted me to "be kind to others," and sometimes that's pretty hard to do and still be truthful. I suspect that they were aware (at some level of consciousness) of the logical conflict in some of these matters, but hadn't really worked it out in their own mind so they never brought it up.

Usually, we manage to sort out the things we were told as children. We cherish the good sense of values we were given, we give "Santa Claus" an appropriate intellectual definition, and, when we discover that our sense of morality is somewhat different from that of our parents, we learn to handle the resultant inner conflicts with a minimum of guilt.

Now I can live with all of that. What really annoys me is when one generation recycles to the next generation a load of plastic concepts that have little relation to the real world, especially when passed on by people who are supposed to know better. I suppose it's excusable and understandable that scholars in the middle ages propagated the idea that the world was flat. They didn't know the facts. But, I have discovered a culprit who passed along to me concepts that should never have been absorbed into the corpus of human knowledge -- MY MUSIC TEACHER.

To be fair, I should probably entertain the possibility that I might have misunderstood him. And I might be inclined to do that, except that when I look at many of the textbooks that are being written today by authorities in music education, I can see that THEIR MUSIC TEACHERS LIED TO THEM, TOO.

My reasons for making this brash accusation are given on the remaining pages of this book. I know it is somewhat presump-tuous of me to challenge the learned scholars of musical academia and the well-established traditions of respected music educators, but -- what the hell.

LIES

MY MUSIC TEACHER
TOLD ME

The world is rich with beautiful music. Composers down through the ages have provided an enormous treasure of musical masterpieces, and these are performed today by thousands of talented musicians, and recorded for our convenience with re-markable fidelity, thanks to fantastic advances made in sound technology during the past few years. The quality and artistry of pop, folk, country and jazz music has reached new standards of excellence. The standards are so high that "stars" without con-siderable talent don't last very long.

But the world is also full of *not* so beautiful music. Who is responsible for that? Does it all come down to "natural talent"? Are some people chosen to be musical artists and the rest relegated to the ranks of the "untalented" by some cosmic decision maker? What can one do to join the ranks of the music *makers* as well as the music consumers. Take music lessons? Go to college?

I wish I could answer with an unequivocal "yes," but I'm afraid I can't. My three and a half decades in musical academia has convinced me that music instruction today is missing the target. Students who developed a musical ear *before* they began formal studies seem to do very well. Those who begin studies "without an ear" tend to drop out in frustration. The major reason this happens is very clear to me. Music teachers tend to start out by teaching *notation* rather than MUSIC. While most college music programs do have classes in ear training, the concepts taught there are usually so naive and removed from the facts of human musical perception that more frustration than enlightenment is generated.

I'm sure you've heard the old saying, "Those who can, do; those who can't, teach." This probably is more true in the arts than in any other field, since artists create their product largely through intuition. While I have known some fine performers who are also great teachers, I have noticed that many super performers have a very difficult time communicating the basics of their craft to beginners. So, even many of the "great ones" tend to teach by parroting the party line of notation. But then, some say that an artist *can't* be taught; he has to learn his art on his own, largely by experimentation.

Well, whether that is true or not, I think music teachers are passing on some very fuzzy, misleading, and sometimes down-right erroneous information about how music works. They undoubtedly got that information from *their* music teachers. So, through the generations, the "talented" students find success and the "untalented" ones find frustration. And teachers probably have basically little to do with either outcome.

To be sure, good teaching inspires success. I'm not talking about that. I'm focusing here on the communication of specific ideas. Can descriptions of artificial musical constructs which ignore the facts of human perception of sound lead students to develop a keener musical awareness? I don't think so. In fact, I think those who do show progress, probably do so in spite of the handicap of being filled with theoretical fiction.

But, could we teachers be more helpful in cultivating the talents of the students who come to us? Yes, I think we could, if we re-examine some of the ideas we have been regurgitating to our students, and would base our educational programs on a sound (in both senses) foundation. I know that asking musicians to recon–sider the major scale is like asking a southern preacher to reconsider the Bible. But that's exactly what I am about to do. (The scale, not the Bible)

The "truths" presented here are practical ones. I am quite familiar with the literature on these subjects, but this is not an academic treatise on music theory, nor is it a textbook. I am simply sharing some ideas that have made sense to me, and which I have used with success. But, as you will see, I do call on the great historical authorities from time to time for their theoretical support. Unfortunately (or perhaps fortunately), they are no longer available to express an endorsements of my ideas, so I guess you'll just have to make up your own mind as to their validity and practicality .

The first part of this book deals with the *pitch* aspect of music and the latter part with the *rhythm* aspect. Each part has a logical continuity, so I suggest you read the chapters in order, rather than thumb ahead to a "lie" that looks particularly interesting. I'm afraid it may not be as clear if read that way.

The book is directed primarily to those who, out of an enthusiastic curiosity about this fascinating art form, began a program of formal study, only to give it up in frustration when the empty rules and artificial constructs failed to reflect the organic lifeblood of music itself. But also, I hope my professional col–leagues in music will consider these ideas, and that this effort might contribute toward making music studies a more successful and satisfying experience.

SCALES, CHORDS, AND OTHER THINGS HAVING TO DO WITH PITCH

Have you ever heard the expression "I can't carry a tune in a basket"? I hate that expression. You hear it all the time when folks are asked to join in a family sing-a-long, or when someone is asked, "How does that tune go?" Now, my music teacher knew that you don't carry tunes in baskets. He believed that you carry them in scales. He said that some melodies were in a "major scale," some were in a "minor scale," and so on. Okay, so it wasn't very funny. But it points to some concepts that I believe have seriously misled us regarding the nature of melodic per—ception and the development of a musical ear.

Sometimes "progress" leads us into some pretty serious situ—ations. The industrial growth of the twentieth century has created a troublesome pollution problem. An altruistic concern for the down-trodden has resulted in young mothers being caught in a "welfare trap."

Music, as well, has suffered from three centuries of "pro–gress." An eighteenth century technological development in keyboard building has progressively dulled our ears and taken away the real "basket" that would have helped us carry our tunes. Instead, we have put our faith in an artificial musical system that bears little relation to the way a human ear organizes musical structures. Why do I think so? Here is why I think so.

Lie #1: Major and minor scales are patterns of pitches arranged in whole steps and half steps, and can be heard by playing them on the piano.

Truth: Major and minor scales are systems of harmonically related pitches, and a piano doesn't play them in tune.

Somewhere in my early music training, I got the impression that a scale was like a row of eggs sitting on a shelf, all more or less equal in importance. Each was named, for convenience, I thought, so we could sing them on *do*, *re*, *mi*, and so on, and thus keep track of where we were in the scale. I'm not sure where I first got this idea, but it may have had to do with how the scale appears when you write it on the staff or play it on the piano.

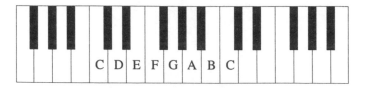

I did notice that when you played a C major scale on a key—board, there were a couple of places where you didn't pass a black note as you went to the next step. My teacher said those were "half steps." I was really delighted when I learned to sing a major scale without the help of the piano, and to recognize one (the scale, not the piano) when I heard it. If someone played a wrong note in the scale I could hear it right away. I didn't know why it was wrong. It just was.

Now that I was hip to the sound of the scale, and knew my *do-re-mi*'s, F♯'s, B♭'s, etc., I should be able to sing music right off the paper. Right??? Wrong!!! Although I could sing the scale from one end to the other, when the music began to skip around, the steps started to sound alike. I kept losing track of where I was in the scale, giving the wrong name to the right pitch and vice versa.

My frustration was magnified when I noticed that there are some people who can identify sound frequencies and can tell, without an instrument, what the pitch name is for a given tone -- B♭, C♯, and so on. This ability, I was told, is a faculty which one either has or hasn't at birth. Traditionally, it has been called "perfect pitch," however a more accurate name is *pitch recognition.*

Well, no matter what you called it, I didn't have it. What's more, I found out that learning perfect pitch is not possible. I have seen some full-page ads in music magazines claiming to teach it; however, I haven't come across any graduates yet. In any case, it's a pretty interesting phenomenon.

A few years ago, I had a student who had "perfect pitch" but grew up using a piano that was badly out of tune. She had identified and labeled all of her pitches considerably lower than standard pitch (A = 440 vibrations per second) and had to trans–pose (mentally change the key) when she sang printed music with a piano or with other people. Now, that's not exactly perfect, is it?

Actually, pitch recognition is a mixed blessing. In my ex–perience with group singers, I have found that people with this "gift" don't always sing in tune as well as those without it. Evidently, when one can produce pitches by frequency perception, one is less likely to depend on the relation of pitches to each other and on matching pitches sung by other people. I guess, if you grew up being the hot-shot music reader in your chorus, and all the other singers followed you, it's a little hard to give that up and surrender to the tuning of other singers.

So, enough of my sour grapes. Since most of us are not able to identify pitches by absolute frequency perception, what are we supposed to do? Leave the music making to the gifted few? The answer, of course, is "no." Nature wisely provided another way. In fact, it is actually a better way (of course I would think so), in that it is related to the physical characteristics of musical sound.

When I grew up, I learned that a scale was not just a "row of eggs," but consists of pitch relationships, and that these can be perceived qualitatively, and that we are able to use a human faculty called a sense of *relative pitch*.. We *all* have this one, and it can be developed to incredible levels of musical awareness. My college teachers knew about relative pitch and provided me with loads of exercises and drills on scales and intervals. But I think they missed the real essence of human pitch perception and how it relates to the way music works. If they did know, they didn't communicate it to me.

Anyway, this is what I have observed about pitch perception over the years. This information would have been helpful during my formative years, and I am quite sure that it will be helpful to anyone hoping to develop a musical ear and gain insight into musical concepts. The ideas here are not particularly original, but seem to have been lost from the mainstream of music instruction over the past few centuries. I think we got hung up on theoretical constructs, like scales, and lost sight of the basic facts of physical sound and our perception of it. I don't know of any beginning music theory textbooks that deal systematically with the *sounds* of music. They all jump right into "this is a quarter note." I believe that music theory makes much more sense after one has some experience with the physical and perceptual nature of musical sound.

The common source of musical sound for educational purposes today is the piano, or its modern offspring, the synthesizer. Now, here is the problem. A keyboard instrument is not capable of delivering accurate pitch information to our ears since it has been tempered, or detuned from natural acoustics, in order to play in all keys. Tempered tuning, developed in the eighteenth century, consists of adjusting the pitches slightly so all the notes -- black and white -- are the same distance apart. This makes it possible for the keyboard to play in any key without retuning. The adjusted intervals, authorities said, are so insig–nificantly altered that the human ear would not be sensitive to the difference. (They lied.)

This event in musical "progress" encouraged music theorists to perpetuate the concept that musical scales are essentially patterns of whole steps and half steps. While a scale may be a pattern of whole steps and half steps as far as the piano is concerned, it is something very different from that when it comes to human perception. Let me explain.

When certain pitches are sounded simultaneously, the combination creates a recognizable quality that human ears can hear and identify. It's something like identifying colors, but not exactly. What is really interesting is that one can hear a given quality even when a different set of pitches is sounded, provided the new set of pitches are the same distance apart as the first set. So, it really is the *relationship* between the pitches that can be identified, not the pitches themselves. Somehow, our brain hears the pitches, compares the frequencies, and sends our consciousness an abstraction, or image, of the physical relationship. Incredible! I don't know how it works, but I know it does.

If you haven't experienced what I'm talking about, try this little experiment. Play a pitch in your medium-low singing range on a sustaining instrument, like an organ or synthesizer. Choose a sound having a simple tone quality, like a flute or string sound, and without vibrato. Now, match your voice to this pitch and then slide your voice up very slowly, like a very lazy siren, and listen to what happens.

If you do it slowly and steadily, you will hear the relationship between the two sounds changing as your voice slides up. It's a bit like tuning in stations on a radio dial (the old fashioned ones that had knobs to turn, not buttons to push). As you arrive at each "local station" it gradually comes into sharp focus and then fades out of focus as you go past it. What you are experiencing is called *consonance* and *dissonance*. When two pitches tend to fuse into each other's frequencies, and seem to agree with each other, they are said to be consonant. To the extent that they don't fuse together and seem to disagree with each other, they are said to be dissonant.

You'll notice that a few pitches are very consonant, others are somewhat consonant, and a few others are rather dissonant but still sound like they relate in some way. It is the differences in the harmonic relationships of this collection of pitches that indicates that a scale is not just a "row of eggs." So, by paying attention to these harmonic qualities, one will eventually learn that each scale step can be recognized by its relationship to a central pitch, called a key, or tonal center. Also, that each scale step has its own personality, and its own set of jobs to do in the major/minor system. That *la* is more than just "a note to follow *so*," and is in fact a note that usually helps determine the mode (major or minor) by providing the color for subdominant harmony, or adds an interesting flavor to tonic harmony, and on some occasions, provides a tasty ninth to a dominant chord. While doing all these different things, *la* manages to retain its own unique personality as "scale step 6." (More about all those technical terms later.)

The reasons why scale step 6 can do all those things can best be understood by knowing something about the physical nature of pitch relations and how that is reflected in our perception of music. Although we don't know exactly how the brain processes the musical raw materials we feed into it, we do know something about the raw materials themselves. Why don't we get down to some basics.

The first musicologist we know much about, the ancient Greek, Pythagoras, viewed music as a branch of mathematics. Now, don't worry. I'm not going to get into a sea of numbers and fancy formulas. The last thing I want is to get bogged in a discussion of "just intonation," "difference tones," "combination tones," etc. If you enjoy that sort of thing, check out any number of marvelous books on the subject at your local library. All I want to do here is demonstrate that musical perception is based on some simple physical facts of harmonic relations that we all can *hear*.

Since Pythagoras had no access to synthesizers, samplers or oscilloscopes, he decided to do something simple--like examine a vibrating string. What he found out was that the string not only vibrated as a whole, creating a basic pitch called the *fundamental*, it also vibrated in halves, thirds, fourths, etc., creating other related pitches, called *partials*. In a sense, this is somewhat like having little pitches within a big pitch. We don't actually hear the little pitches individually. They vary in strength from one sound source to another to create what we hear as *timbre*, or tone quality. It's what makes a trumpet sound different from a violin. But we *can* hear the relationship that occurs when a second audible pitch is sounded at the frequency of one of these partials. We just ob–served that in our experiment above.

So, let's take a closer look at the relationship between the vibrating string and the perceptual comparison of related pitches. Everytime a whole string moves back and forth one time, each half of the string moves back and forth twice. In other words, the half string is moving twice as fast as the whole string. This means that not only is the pitch of the half string higher than the pitch of the whole string, but it is related in a simple way to the pitch of the whole string. We can express the relationship of the two pitches as a ratio of one to two (or 1:2). What is rather remarkable is that we mere mortals are equipped to hear this relationship. We can't count the vibrations, but we can tell when two pitches are sounding in this relationship.

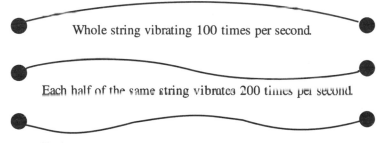

Whole string vibrating 100 times per second.

Each half of the same string vibrates 200 times per second.

Each third of the same string vibrates 300 times per second.

We can also hear the relationship between a pitch cor–responding to the whole string and a pitch corresponding to a *third* of the string (1:3). Other simple ratios can also be easily heard, and with a bit of concentrated practice one can learn to hear and identify pitch relationships as high as the 13th partial or so.

Now, we don't need a real string in order to experience this perceptual phenomenon. The sound of the two pitches can come from any source, and eventually, as with any concept, these "sounds" can exist purely in the imagination. Beethoven didn't have to stop composing after he became deaf. He already knew what pitches went together how, and also what they sounded like. In other words, he had developed a "sound vocabulary" of pitch relationships.

Remember, we don't need to know the names of individual pitches in order to experience and recognize a specific relationship between them. Most of us can't identify frequencies anyway. What we *can* perceive and re-create are the relationships them–selves, and with a bit of training can learn to recognize and name them.

When you were using the sliding technique described earlier, you probably discovered a number of pitches that seem to agree (in varying amounts) with your sustained low note. If you selected C as your low note, the most "agreeable" pitches you found were probably on white notes on the keyboard, and likely included these:

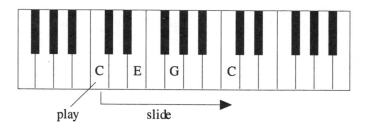

Try it again and as you find a consonant pitch in your voice, find it on the keyboard. If you listen carefully, you will notice that most of the keyboard notes are slightly different from the pitches you are singing. That's because the keyboard is tempered tuned and you're not.

Consonance and dissonance are relative terms, that is, various intervals can be very consonant, somewhat consonant, rather dissonant, very dissonant, or various shades in between. However, consonance is not like light, in that one can increase light in a gradual continuum (in shades of gray from black to blinding). When you combine two voices on the exact same pitch, or in a 1:1 ratio (a perfect consonance), and then move one voice to the pitch that creates the next most simple ratio (which would be 1:2), you have to jump to another location in the scale rather than going gradually through "shades" of consonance, like light.

Let me show you what I mean. Let's say you started your slide (in the experiment above) on the pitch C. While your voice was in unison with the instrument, you had a 1:1 ratio. As you made your voice slide up, you would not reach the 1:2 ratio until you moved all the way up to the next C on the instrument. (It's called an octave because it encompasses eight scale steps.) If C makes the high note too high for your voice, try it on any lower note. It will work on any pitch.

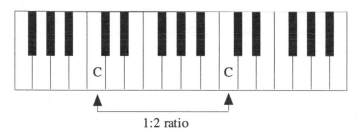

1:2 ratio

Now try this. Sustain the low note on the instrument and sing the 1:2 ratio note (an octave) above. While sustaining the high note, move your voice very slightly away from that pitch, both up and down. Notice that this creates considerable dissonance. When your voice is in the center of the area of agreement, you are "in tune." When you hear the noisy conflict of disagreement, you are "out of tune." Once you get the idea, you no longer need to ask an expert whether you are in or out of tune. Your ear tells you.

Before we go on, I want you to notice that not only do both pitches in a 1:2 ratio have the same letter name, but logically all higher multiples (2, 4, 8, 16, etc.), since they are all in 1:2 ratios, will have that letter name as well. Also, partial 3 will have the same letter name as partials 6, 12, 24, etc. What this means is that an interval can be "measured" perceptually by the nearest repre‐sentatives of the pitch names concerned. For example, a 2:3 ratio is essentially the same as a 1:3 ratio since partial 2 has the same name as the fundamental. Okay, let's go on.

So where is the next most consonant interval? Our tuning experiment demonstrated that it is clearly not *near* the pitch that gave us our 1:2 ratio. Logic tells us that it would be a ratio of 1:3, and the third partial would be higher than the second partial, so we are probably running out of vocal range. Now here is where we can use the information in the preceding paragraph. To keep things within a manageable range, we will use partial 2 as our "fundamental" and slide up from there. We find the pitch we're looking for slightly higher than halfway up the octave. If your low note was C, the upper pitch of the 2:3 ratio is on the high side of the keyboard's G. It fairly jumps out at you when you find it. I have observed that most students learn to produce and recognize this interval with relative ease.

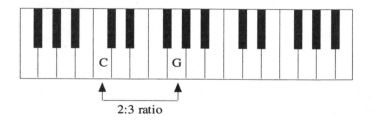

2:3 ratio

If we chart the first six (most consonant) partials of the pitch C on the keyboard, showing their ratios to the fundamental, we see that they represent only three different pitch names--C, E, and G.

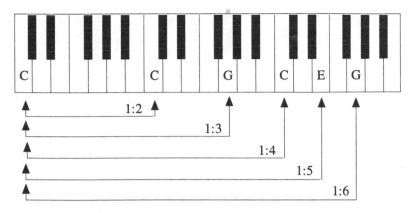

A convenient (and ultimately more useful) way to show these relationships is by the ratios of neighboring partials, as we did with the perfect fifth above.

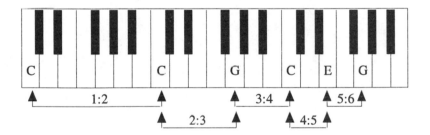

You may already know that these pitches are collectively called a *major chord*. Each of the three members has its own functional name while in this relationship. The C, being the fundamental pitch from which the others are derived, is called the *root*. The E is called the *third*, because it occurs on the third scale step above the C root. And G is called the *fifth* for similar reasons.

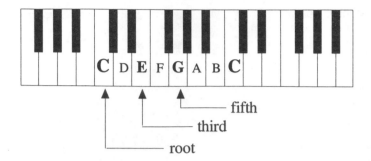

You may also know that it doesn't matter in what order or spacing the three pitches appear, because it is the *harmonic relationship* of the pitches that creates that particular musical construct and provides that unique perceptual experience. Like a family sitting around the dinner table, Dad is still Dad no matter where he sits. (In the interest of avoiding all those cards, letters and phone calls, Mom is still Mom, too.)

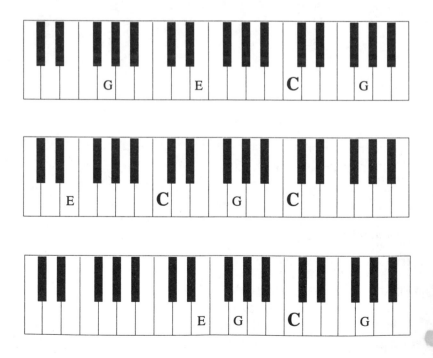

A major chord, like all perceptual Gestalts, is something other than the sum of its parts. Only when all three members are present (actually or in imagination) does the concept exist. It is an abstraction--an idea--as well as a physical phenomenon. When considered separately, each of the pitches C, E and G are independent in importance and significance. But when considered together as a harmonic family, C is always the boss. Just as Pythagoras' partials were generated by a fundamental pitch, the frequency of a root determines the tuning of its "satellite" pitches.

Let's extend our chart of the pitches in Pythagoras' string to include others beyond the first six partials. Please remember, however, that this keyboard representation is only an approximation of the real pitches

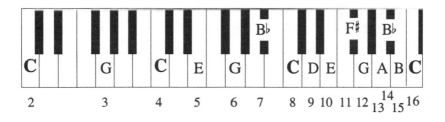

Notice that the distance between partials gets smaller as the numbers get higher--1:2 is an octave (eight scale steps), 2:3 is a fifth (five scale steps), 3:4 is a fourth, and so on. Since that principle continues up the series of partials, the interval between G and B♭ (6:7) is actually smaller than the interval between E and G (5:6). On the keyboard, both these thirds contain one and a half steps, and they sound identical in harmonic relationship when you play them. Clearly, the keyboard is not telling the truth here. But then you noticed that it wasn't a model of veracity in its performance of a perfect fifth either (2:3).

What this means in practical terms is that, while G tunes acoustically to a C root slightly higher than piano pitch, the acoustic B♭ will tune somewhat lower than piano pitch. This, in turn, makes the interval from that B♭ up to C (7:8) a larger whole step than the one from C to D (8:9), and both of those are larger than the whole step from D to E (9:10).

At this point you may be thinking, "Is this really important? Does anyone really care?" Well, I suppose it's not as important as finding a soul mate, inventing electricity or establishing world peace. It's only important if you like your music to be in tune. You also may be thinking, "Can one really hear the difference?" Well, let's find out.

Play a C on a sustaining keyboard and sing G, moving it up and down until you hear it lock in. Then play G on the keyboard and you will hear the difference. If it sounds the same to you, you're probably not singing high enough to hear pure tuning. Now, do the same on B♭ (remember, it's lower than piano pitch) while playing a C root. Pretty interesting, don't you think?

So, the problem with the keyboard was that the partials (or intervalic relationships between pitches) don't line up when you play in different keys. If you tuned the instrument acoustically on a C fundamental, you might tolerate the tuning on a closely related root like G or F. But if you played in a more distantly related key, like E or F♯, it would sound pretty awful. So, from the keyboardist's standpoint, tempered tuning was a terrific thing. And it would have been a terrific thing for the rest of us, too, had we been warned during our formative years regarding these natural facts of life. Instead, we got the plastic information.

But this has been going on for a very long time. Hermann Helmholtz, a very prominent nineteenth century writer on musical acoustics, had complaints on the subject:

> That performers of the highest rank do really play in just in-
> tonation, has been directly proved by the very interesting and exact

results of Delezenne (1826). This observer determined the individual notes of the major scale, as it was played by distinguished violinist and violoncellists, by means of an accurately gauged string, and found that these players produced correctly perfect Thirds and Sixths, and neither equally tempered nor Pythagorean Thirds or Sixths. I was fortunate enough to have an opportunity of making similar observations by means of my harmonium on Herr Joachim. He tuned his violin exactly with the g+d+a+e of my instrument. I then requested him to play the scale, and immediately he had played the Third or Sixth, I gave the corresponding note on the harmonium. By means of beats it was easy to determine that this distinguished musician used b^1 and not b as the major third to g, and e^1 not e as the Sixth.

But if the best players who are thoroughly acquainted with what they are playing are able to overcome the defects of their school and of the tempered system, it would certainly wonderfully smooth the path of performers of the second order, in their attempts to attain a perfect *ensemble*, if they had been accustomed from the first to play the scales by natural intervals. The greater trouble attending the first attempts would be amply repaid by the result when the ear has once become accustomed to hear perfect consonances. It is really much easier to apprehend the differences between notes of the same name in just intonation than people usually imagine, when the ear has once become accustomed to the effect of just consonances. (*On The Sensations Of Tone*, 1863. English translation, Ellis, 1875. p. 325)

I guess nobody listened. Maybe Helmholtz needed a more effective press agent. But he is absolutely right about purely tuned pitch relations being *easier* to perceive, and thereby conceive. Intervals become unique, and therefore more recognizable; and as a result, mushy tempered-tuned melodies are replaced by sparkling ones

So, now that you know the difference, you have a choice to make. Which world of music do *you* want to exist in? I probably should have warned you that once exposed to hearing pure tuning you may never again be able to sing or play comfortably with other people who don't understand this kind of harmonic sensitivity. I get "complaints" every January from my L.A. Jazz Choir singers who do holiday caroling with other vocal groups

I tell them, as I suggest to you, to pass the word along. There is a better world of harmonic awareness. We didn't invent it. It's a part of nature. It just got lost along the way.

Lie #2: Singing along with the piano will help to develop an accurate sense of pitch.

Truth: Singing along with the piano will tend to prevent the development of an accurate sense of pitch.

The invention of tempered tuning, as exciting as it was for eighteenth century harpsichordists and for every keyboardist since, was for the rest of us a mixed blessing. As we noted earlier, in order to build keyboards that can play in any key, it is necessary to slightly adjust all the pitches between the octaves. Paul Hindemith seemed to think that this was not a problem.

> Singers and players of wind and string instruments use untempered tuning. Guided by the ear, they dispose of the (discrepancy) by always seeking to produce harmonic intervals in their simplest form . (*The Craft of Musical Composition*, 1937)

Mr. Hindemith must have been listening to different singers and players than I. Most of the singers and players I come across don't even know there *is* a difference between keyboard tuning and "pure" tuning -- even some educated ones. When the subject came up at all during my education, we were assured that the slight difference in pitch was probably not significant to the human ear, and even if it was, our musical sensibilities would correct the discrepancy. Let me tell you, IT DIDN'T HAPPEN!

It might have happened had we made sure that young ears had ample opportunity to hear untempered, pure intervals. Instead, the keyboards won out and we now have a population of music makers who can't hear pure pitch relations. Our choirs can't sing in tune. Our solo singers swim through melodies with the hope that they are somewhere near the pitch. Over the years, our ears have heard tempered fifths, thirds and seconds until they sound "right." Last week, I came across a veteran piano-bar singer who insisted that the pure intervals we were singing "sounded sharp" to her.

Choral singers almost universally "learn their notes" in tempered tuning. The altos practice their part by hearing it drummed out on the old eighty-eight. Then they sing their mushy conception along with the mushy conceptions of the sopranos, tenors and basses. The result, as we all painfully know, is fre– quently an ugly conglomeration of sounds only a proud mother could tolerate. It's no wonder that so many choruses can't main– tain pitch when they sing *a cappella* (without instruments). Their dependence on the keyboard is so strong that when it is not playing they are tonally adrift.

Having worked with professional singers, I have to say that most (yes, most) formally trained singers (even those with graduate degrees) have never really experienced pure acoustic pitch relationships. Their ears are corrupted by years of practicing scales and chords with a tempered-tuned piano (or worse, an out-of-tune piano). Most can't produce a purely-tuned perfect fifth -- one of the simplest of harmonic relationships. String and wind players have a much better circumstance for learning accurate tuning simply because they do their practicing without a keyboard. Mother Nature is more likely to be heard when she doesn't have to shout through artificial tuning.

Again, this is not a new situation. Another quote from the nineteenth century acoustician, Helmholtz:

It is impossible not to acknowledge that at the present day few even of our opera singers are able to execute a little piece for several voices, when either totally unaccompanied, or at most accompanied by occasional chords...in a manner suited to give the hearer a full enjoyment of its perfect harmony.... But where are our singers to learn just intonation and make their ears sensitive for perfect chords? They are from the first taught to sing to the equally-tempered piano–forte.... The singer who practises to a tempered instrument has no principle at all for exactly and certainly determining the pitch of his voice.

On the other hand, we often hear four musical amateurs who have practised much together, singing quartetts in perfectly just intonation. Indeed, my own experience leads me almost to affirm that quartetts are more frequently heard with just intonation when sung by young men who scarcely sing anything else, and often and regularly practise them, than when sung by instructed solo singers who are accustomed to the accompaniment of the pianoforte or the orchestra. (*On The Sensation Of Tone*, p. 326)

Helmholtz, if he were alive today, would very likely champion an American amateur singing tradition that is frequently frowned on by academia. Have you ever heard a really good barbershop chorus? Barbershoppers can "bust a chord" that is absolutely thrilling. Every voice is focused into and absorbed by the sound until the product becomes something more than the sum of the parts. A well-tuned vocal chord is something that an individual cannot create by himself. It takes a number of individuals, each voluntarily giving up his individuality for the sake of a common experience. Boy, I *like* that!

And, guess what! NO PIANOS ALLOWED. The only instrument in a barbershop rehearsal is a pitch pipe. A single pitch is given, everyone hums his note in *relation* to the given pitch, and away they go. And guess what else. They don't go flat! (Unless they have poor vocal production, which they often do. But that's another book. It will be titled *Components of Vocal Blend*. Watch for it at your local book store.)

I won't go so far as to recommend that pianos be banned from elementary school classrooms, but I would suggest that young–sters *learn* vocal music without a keyboard. Then, after they have experienced the pitches in relation to each other, accompany with the piano when appropriate. Interestingly, the tempered tuning of the keyboard doesn't seem to bother choral tuning once it is locked in place. The same is true for solo singing. The end result is simply a more sparkling musical product.

Evidently the quick decay in the loudness of struck strings keeps the piano sound in the background when sounding along with a sustained voice. Also, the timbres, or tone qualities, of voice and piano are not at all similar. Guitar, too, although tem–pered, would be an effective alternative for vocal accompani–ment. These characteristics are, of course, not true of the organ, and singing against such sustained tempered pitches does cause considerable problems, particularly in slow-moving passages.

In this regard, Jim Mooney, one of the finest recording engineers in Los Angeles, and I were sitting in the golf cart discussing vocal and piano tuning while waiting to tee off. He brought up an interesting point: good piano accompanists know better than to play the melody with the soloist. I had always believed that this was to avoid tying up the soloist, leaving him free to phrase around the beat with a graceful rubato. Jim pointed out that another reason is probably that playing the melody in tempered tuning would either fight with the soloist's flexible tuning or pull him into tempered pitch. The result would be either annoying dissonances or dull and boring melodies, or perhaps a bit of both. A good point!

As I am writing this, I am trying to remember when I became aware of the piano's detrimental effect on well-tuned singing. I remember some great sounds when I was a singer in the Royal Oak (Michigan) High School A Cappella Choir. Mr. Feighner would have the basses establish a solid starting pitch and we would build chords, adding one note at a time and listening carefully to make sure it fit exactly into the sound. That choir sang some great music, but what I remember most is the tuning warm-up. Now, *that* music teacher was not lying. Perhaps this was the seed that later flowered and helped me escape the tempered-tuning bondage that seems to enslave most of today's singers. Like most young students of great teachers, I took my training for granted, thinking that all high school singers were learning the same things we were. Boy, was I wrong!

A related incident happened some years later in a choral conducting class at Indiana University. I had just sung a phrase to illustrate some point, and the instructor informed me that I had sung it sharp. It wasn't really a big deal to me at the time, but it did stick in my mind over the years and caused me to take special care that I didn't sing sharp. I wish I could go back in time and hear me sing that phrase again. I would really like to know whether I actually was singing sharp, or whether my high-school training caused me to sing some of the notes in the phrase higher than that teacher was used to hearing them. My suspicion that the latter was true is significantly intensified as I remember that he was a "neck-tie" baritone who frequently sang *lower* than piano pitch. So, who knows? Maybe I was sharp. And then again, maybe that teacher was operating with tempered ears.

During the early years of my career as a music educator, I slipped away from my solid high school training in fine tuning. I fell in with the crowd, pounding out notes on the piano for my choirs and settling for "vicinity" tuning like most everyone else. Most group singing I heard was so bad that anything that approxi–mated piano pitch was considered a success. I was also probably distracted from tuning because I was trying out all those "choral techniques" I had learned in college.

It wasn't until I was teaching the Pierce College Jazz Choir that I realized how detrimental the piano was to developing accurate pitch concepts. I had known (as do most music educators) about tempered tuning, but had been unconcerned (as are most music educators) about its effect on accurate tuning. Now it was bugging me that these kids couldn't make the hot jazz chords "pop." The music sounded dumpy and "square." (There is nothing more lame than a poorly-tuned thirteenth-flat-nine chord.) Being a *Hi-Los* fan, I knew these chords could be much more exciting.

So, I suggested to Dwight, our accompanist, to play only the roots as we sang our up-a-fifth warm-ups. This exercise was very beneficial in demonstrating what "in tune" really meant. When fifths were secure, we moved on to other intervals until the singers could make a minor second (half step) sparkle like a musical diamond.

Dwight Elrich is one of the finest accompanists I have ever worked with. He has great ears. Often he hears clinkers in the sound that I miss. He is much more than a piano player.

So with Dwight's help, we weaned our Pierce College Jazz Choir singers away from tempered tuning. When we tuned chords, he played only the root note and allowed the singer to find the place where the notes locked into place. Our motto was "sing *into* the chord, not through it." (We also focused on some other things that helped us to sing "into" chords; like vowel focus, neutral syllables, resonance matching, brightness agreement. But that's another book. Watch for it at your local... Oh, we did that already, didn't we?).

The focus on tuning paid off bigger than we could have ever imagined. Our audiences grew beyond Mom, Pop and Uncle Bill. Jim Washburn, then a producer at KCET, the Los Angeles PBS station, invited the group to do a sixty-minute television special. We participated in the Playboy Jazz Festival, singing at the mansion for the press conference and opening the show that year at the Hollywood Bowl. After a trip to the European Jazz festivals in Montreux and The Hague, we recorded an album which got us a Grammy nomination. Pretty heady stuff for a bunch of college kids, wouldn't you say?

The biggest problem we had was that the graduating singers wouldn't leave the group and new students couldn't get into it. After they graduated from Pierce College, they went on to USC or Cal State Northridge or got jobs, but made sure they could still schedule Pierce College Jazz Choir. So we quit calling it a college group and those singers became "pros" (if you call ten bucks a gig a living). Thus, in 1980 the L.A. Jazz Choir was born.

Soon, singers were coming from all over town to audition for the L.A. Jazz Choir, including some experienced professional singers. That was terrific, we thought at first, but it introduced a new problem. The new singers were not always hip to the vocal techniques that had brought the group to prominence. Most were locked into "piano tuning," unfocused vowels, and other vocal habits that the group had overcome. This, of course, annoyed the veterans. It annoyed them even more that it took up precious rehearsal time to make the new singers aware of "acoustic tuning" and other basic requisites for making the LAJC sound.

So we established the L.A. Jazz Choir Workshop, where singers new to the organization could hone the needed skills as well as learn the LAJC book. Here the new singers could explore jazz style, tuning, blend and phrasing without the pressure of a performance schedule, and without slowing down the LAJC performing group's rehearsal.

You may be wondering, "Why all this background on the L.A. Jazz Choir?" Actually, I have a point. Let me make it by describing a typical (and quite frequent) moment in a workshop session. We're trying to get a chord to lock and we've checked vowels, resonance and other enemies of blend but it just won't happen. We'd check each chord member by having Dwight sustain the root and have all the singers on that note adjust it until all the noise (dissonant "beats") disappears. If it still doesn't happen, we go down the line having each singer tune individually. The stubborn pitch is frequently (but not always) coming from one of the new kids on the block. The other singers in the room are feeling and acting like revival-meeting zealots knowing that a new convert is about to be born into the kingdom.

As I work with the new singer, urging him to forsake the security of piano pitch, suggesting he risk being sharp "just to see what happens," the other singers are offering encouragement like, "Go ahead," "Try it," "You'll see," etc. At first the prospective "convert" is reluctant and confused and is convinced that we are all a little crazy for asking him to sing the pitch out of tune. Eventually this defensiveness is replaced by curiosity, and finally the singer begins to explore the space outside his old comfort zone. When he experiences the peaceful calm that occurs when the note locks with Dwight's sustained root, the eyebrows raise, the eyes widen, giving evidence that another soul has been saved from the fuzziness of tempered tuning.

It is probably gratifying for the new singer to notice all the smiles in the room, and it must be reinforcing when the smiles appear precisely at the moment of successful tuning. To be honest, however, I'm not sure that all of the smiles are a result of happiness for the singer's new musical life. I suspect that some part of the joy comes from the knowledge that we won't have to listen to that singer's tempered tuning anymore.

Lie #3: Singing scales and melodies is the best way to begin the development of a musical ear.

Truth: Developing accuracy in melodic skills depends greatly on a sense of harmonic reslationships.

So, which came first--melody or harmony? Alhough it may look like the old "chicken or egg" question, it really isn't. History indicates that melody was far more prevalent in early musical traditions of the world. In fact, Western European culture is the only one that "went harmonic." Most of the others developed highly sophisticated melodic subtleties and/or rhythmic complexities. This fact evidently has influenced music educators to assume that, since melody came first historically, melody should be the first item of business in training musical ears.

As you might expect, I have a serious problem with that philosophy. An examination of the structure of most melodic traditions shows that the pitches in a given system (or *scale*) are almost always based on harmonic considerations. I'm not suggesting that *all* melody is based on pure harmonic relationships. Arnold Schoenberg and his disciples composed music on an artificial system (twelve equally spaced pitches) and achieved an interesting, if not charming, result. But have you noticed how popular that systems is today? Have you ever tried to sing twelve-tone music? Have you ever tried to *listen* to it?

I know this discussion is making me vulnerable to the charge that I am obviously incapable of appreciating the more chal‐lenging styles of musical creation. If that's what you are thinking, you are in fact making my point. The main reason these artificial musical systems are more challenging is because THEY ARE ARTIFICIAL SYSTEMS. That is, they are based on a mathe‐matical divison of the octave into equal segments rather than on the small-number ratios of natural perceptual harmonics.

So whether or not all melody is based on harmonic rela‐tionships is not the point here. It really doesn't matter. What does matter is that melody *can* be perceived (and measured) in terms of harmonic vocabulary. Even twelve-tone music. In fact, a sense of relative pitch (harmonic relationships) is the *only perceptual means* of accurate melodic measurement we humans have (except for "those" people). When one considers that harmonic perceptions are based on observable physical facts (remember Pythagoras' string) it makes even more sense. I *know*, after thirty five years of teaching ear training, that music students who know their way around a major chord are better at singing melodies accurately than those who don't. *Especially* Schoenberg's melodies.

The important question here, then, is not which came first historically, but rather "how and to what extent do melodic structures derive from harmonic relationships?" We can begin finding our answer by noting that the melodic perfect fifth interval is found prominently in ethnic musical systems around the world. A few years ago, I did a musicological study for a lawyer who wanted to know how "original" the *March of the Winkies* was (from *The Wizard of Oz*). As you may remember, the tune is a chantlike melody which consists entirely of perfect fifths.

Oh - ee - oh,   Ee - oh._____

Since I suspected that fifths were pretty basic to most all musical systems, I went down to the UCLA ethnomusicology library and listened to music from every corner of the world. What I heard verified that the perfect fifth is to melody what the two-by-four is to house building. Without this basic stabilizing ingre-dient, melody would lose perceptual focus and become a rather mushy affair. And that is roughly what melody appears to be for many music students who haven't developed harmonic awareness --a mushy affair.

Now here's a critical point. People don't always know why they think what they think. That's why we need psychiatrists, sociologists and psychologists. Just because the world was full of melody before it was full of harmony doesn't mean that a human sense of harmonic relations was not influencing the way melodies were put together. Just because the early music theorists talked almost exclusively about melodic practice doesn't mean that acoustical considerations had no effect on melodic creation. Ex-amination of the melodic product itself shows that the contrary is quite likely true.

It is very significant that the earliest harmony, in the eighth or ninth century, was created at the interval of a perfect fifth. Rumor has it that a high-ranking clergyman was inadvertently singing the tune a fifth lower than the others and no one had the nerve to draw it to his attention. Although that story is probably suspect, the fact that the world's first harmony occurred at the interval of a fifth is not. Pythagoras wouldn't have been surprised. He'd have con-sidered the "out of tune" clergyman a clever and perceptive chap.

This breakthrough in musical practice provided a new way of making musical compositions. The new music consisted of com-bining simultaneous melodies related at structural points by the stability of the perfect fifth and other consonant intervals. On the surface it appeared that "harmony was born." Actually it had been there all the time, probably influencing how melody had been shaped all through the earlier centuries.

Formal music during the early centuries in Europe was largely religious and was based on a few scales called *church modes*. All of the church modes can be found on the white notes of the modern keyboard (approximately, of course). Each mode was characterized by a different pattern of whole steps and half steps. However, notice that a feature common to all of these modes is the perfect fifth interval occuring from step 1 to step 5.

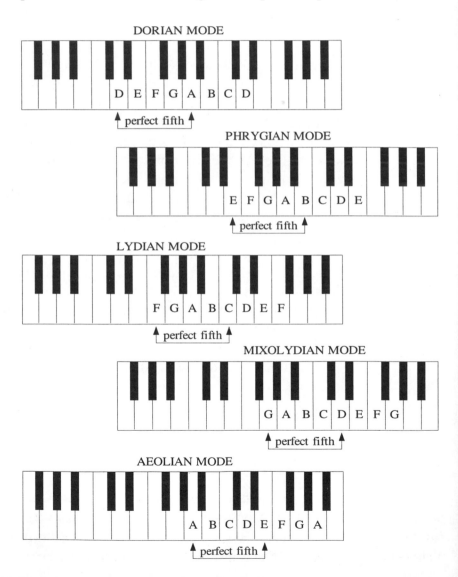

It is significant that the whole-step/half-step pattern from B to B was *not* used by the musical church fathers. Notice that it is the only white-note scale pattern on the keyboard that doesn't have a perfect fifth between scalesteps 1 and 5. It's smaller than the others. There are only two black notes between, instead of three. Play it. You'll hear the difference.

LOCRIAN MODE

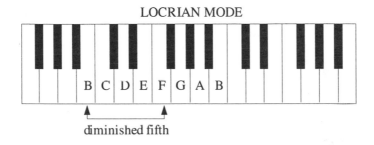

diminished fifth

One has to believe that the B mode was not used because of this unstable fifth between scalesteps one and five. Interestingly, composers struggled with this strange fifth all through the early centuries of musical development. It wasn't until the seventeenth century, just before the time of J. S. Bach, that composers figured out how to deal with it. Their revelations introduced the world to the most incredible musical construct ever devised (discovered?)-- the major/minor system.

The great eighteenth century theorist, Jean-Philippe Rameau, proposed what was then a very novel idea: that all music is founded on *harmony*. His conclusions arose from a consideration of natural principles of math and physical vibrating bodies. Seems like a reasonable thing to do, doesn't it? Pythagoras would have thought so.

Rameau suggested that this new system of making music was based on a brand new concept--*chords*. Yes, it's hard to believe, but the concept of these basic building blocks of musical structure that we take for granted today is actually only about four hundred years old. Before chords, musicians thought of music as a horizontal (melodic) flow, sometimes with simultaneous lines connected at critical points by stable intervals. Now we think of music as having both horizontal (melodic) and vertical (harmonic) aspects.

A significant part of Rameau's work was that it explained, to a great extent, how that non-perfect fifth in the B mode works. The early church musicians were thinking of it basically in melodic terms. By viewing this unstable interval harmonically, its use becomes clear and practical. You can be sure that we will want to talk more about that later.

The import of Rameau's revelations evidently has been lost on today's music educators. It appears that they are more influenced by the historical order of musical development. Since melody "came first," it was apparently assumed that one should study music and train young ears by concentrating on melody first. I think we followed the wrong path.

In my experience as a teacher, I have observed that melodies are too complex for a novice ear to grasp in a structural way. Swimming teachers wouldn't throw their new students into the deep end of the pool, but I'm afraid music teachers do. While drowning in a swirl of pitches may not be detrimental to one's physical well being, it can be very devastating to a young person's musical growth. If his confidence was wavering before he tackled scale singing, the experience could supply the fatal blow, and relegate him to the ranks of those who believe they can't carry a tune in a you-know-what.

I am convinced that the way to understanding melodic struc–ture is to first understand how scalesteps relate *harmonically* to a central pitch, or tonic note. Once that happens, individual scale–steps will take on a "personality" that can be identified and/or produced at will and with confidence. The "eggs in a row" concept of scales is gone. Singing no longer swims around the pitches, but sparkles with a focused relationship to a central tonic. Music reading becomes a translation of symbols that represent REAL MUSICAL PERCEPTIONS AND CONCEPTS instead of an insecure guessing game.

Helmholz seems to believe that accurate harmonic concepts provide the basis for accurate melodic performance. (I'm really getting to like this guy.)

> The relations of the tones are generally much easier to feel with distinctness in harmonised than in homophonic (he means *unharmonized*) music. In the latter the feeling of relationship of tone depends solely on the sameness of pitch of two partials in two consecutive musical tones. But when we hear the second ...tone we can at most remember the first, and hence we are driven to complete the comparison by an act of memory. The consonance, on the other hand, gives the relation by an immediate act of sensation; we are no longer driven to have recourse to memory; we hear beats, or there is a roughness in the combined sound, when the proper relations are not preserved. (*On The Sensation Of Tone*, p. 292)

In other words, practice with *simultaneous* pitches provides the basis for practice with pitches sounded one after the other. Once we get used to hearing how pitches sound together, we can learn to *remember* the overtone structure of the first pitch and compare it to the second pitch. We can also learn to *anticipate* where the second pitch will go while singing the first one.

Doesn't it make sense to start with the simplest things to hear-- pure, simple intervals--and build from there. Doesn't it seem logical if we want to teach people how music works, to start by demonstrating the *basic stuff* of which major/minor music is made? Like chords? "What!!!" I can hear some readers gasping. "Teach chords before scales? Never! It just isn't done!" I know. That's the problem!

Happily, I ran across a new ear-training textbook recently that introduced the major chord as a basic structural concept in the *second* chapter (although there was no discussion of acoustical relationships). Interestingly, the first chapter still dealt with the obligatory discussion of wholesteps and halfsteps, an aural perception that, in my teaching experience, is one of the most difficult to develop. I suspect that the author knows that the major chord is a good place to start, but also knows that if he doesn't put scales up front many music teachers won't use his book.

Melodies in major and minor modes are usually conceived from harmonic structures. In other words, the selection of melodic pitches is greatly influenced by the chords the composer has in mind as he composes his tune. Since this is true, one would think that music educators should begin the musical development of their students by providing a well-constructed harmonic "basket" in which to carry the tune. My teacher didn't. And I suspect yours didn't either.

Lie #4: Naming scale steps on syllables (do, re, mi, etc.) or numbers (1, 2, 3, etc.) will lead to success in singing melodies accurately.

Truth: Naming things does not contribute to identifying them when the "things" have not been previously experienced as unique, and therefore are un-namable.

The use of syllables in teaching melodic skills is almost as old as the Bible and is often practiced as religiously. It was invented by Guido of Arezzo in the tenth century and has been very widely used since then. As melodies became more chromatic, the system was improved on, adding syllables to represent the "black notes" as well as the "white notes." Some teachers use the syllables to represent fixed pitches (*do* is always C, *fa* is always F, *me* is always E♭, etc.), while others use the syllables to represent the relational aspects of scale steps in any key (*do* is always scale step 1, *fa* is always 4, *se* is always ♭5, etc.)

Other teachers (including me) have preferred numbers over syllables, mainly because it means one less new language to learn. Students are already familiar with the order of the numbers from one to seven, so I prefer not to bother with *do-re-mi*'s. (Sorry, Guido).

There are some disadvantages, however, in using numbers instead of syllables. For example, "seven" has two syllables, so it's awkward to sing it on one note. I sort of scrunch it into a one syllable sound--"sev'n"--and it works pretty well. Also, when you sing a chromatic pitch, you have to call it "sharp five" or the like, and it gets pretty awkward sometimes.

In actual practice the awkwardness is not really a problem. Once a student catches on to the sounds of the basic scale steps, he really doesn't need to name out loud everything he sings. In fact, trying to name every note gets in the way once he works up a little speed. For example, a scalewise passage only requires the identification of a starting and ending place. And even then, the starting and ending places don't require audible identification--just thinking the concept is all that is needed. When you see someone whose name you can't recall, it doesn't mean you don't recognize him. Of course it would be awkward to say, "Hi, there, person whom I met on the golf course the other day." But you knew who he was even though you didn't say his name.

I suppose the decision to use one system or the another depends largely on what the teacher expects the naming to ac–complish. If syllables are only intended to provide convenient names by which to refer to specific pitches, then "fixed *do*" is perfectly adequate. This system can't help us very much in devel–oping an aural sense of musical organization, however, since most of us mortals don't recognize fixed pitches (frequencies) anyway.

If labels are intended to refer to tonal relationships, then either "moveable *do*" or numbers is useful. If the goal is to name every note one sings, then learning Guido's syllables would be the logical choice. If one needs only occasionally to name a specific scale step, thinking of most notes as belonging to larger concepts (like scales, or chords), then numbers are just fine.

But, here's the problem with syllables and numbers. It's not that they are used in teaching melody, but that teachers seem to believe (or at least imply to students) that the use of syllables (or numbers) in itself leads to success in *recognizing* scale steps. I don't think it does.

I have seen some musicians who can rip through some pretty tough melodies at sight who swear by syllables, and others who are pretty decent with numbers. What caused me to become suspicious was observing students who sang correct pitches and called them by wrong names. It was clear to me that it was not the names that led students to the right pitches. They learned the system in spite of the names. They could have sung "dum-da-dum-da-dum" or "scoo-be-doo-be-doo" and done just as well.

Actually, we probably learn everything in spite of the names. In fact, sometimes a name sends us down the wrong trail and confuses us until we discover the erroneous assumption. So that brings us to the central question: Why do some of us sing accurately and in tune and some of us can't find the basket?

I think part of the answer has to do with paying attention to the right things, and doing it before we are confused with *do-re-mi*'s, F-sharps and flat-sevens. Can you imagine someone learning to walk by reading a book? Or learning to speak by looking at letters? Of course not. We learn to walk by experiencing the dynamics of bodily movement. We learn to speak by imitating sounds. And, just as naturally, we learn musical structures by experiencing and imitating pitch relations.

Sara McFerrin, Bobby's mother, was telling us at a music educators convention that, during his very early years, he would hang around under the piano while she was giving music lessons. He would make these funny little sounds with his voice, exploring with eager curiosity the possibilities of pitch combinations. Today, Bobby McFerrin is recognized as the most phenomenal vocal "gymnast" in the world, and probably, in musical history.

It is not surprising that music students with the best ears come from families where music was happening as a normal part of life. Youngsters who were encouraged to participate in music making at a young age seem to have gotten it together somehow. Some of these "together" kids eventually find their way into college music classes and simply have to learn the names for what they already know. Other students in the same classes struggle with the *do-re-mi*'s and 1-2-3's hoping that these labels will unlock the tonal mysteries that seem to elude them. Happily, breakthroughs do occur, and that brings hope to others who want earnestly to join the "musical people."

Let me make sure that you get my point. Musical literacy is not merely reading and writing musical notation just as language literacy is not merely putting words into syntax. True literacy, in either sense, is making connections between symbols and ideas. In music, ideas are conceptual patterns of sound. Without the sounds, notation is essentially meaningless.

Musical sounds seem to "swim" in the perception of many people -- even some musically educated people. These folks simply never developed an awareness of the pure and simple stuff that music is made of. Future architects play with blocks, Tinker-Toys and Lego sets. Future artists play with pencils, crayons and paint books. Future poets play with words, feelings and ideas. Future musicians (amateur or professional) need to play with pitches.

But, how? It's pretty unlikely that a youngster will get excited about the sounds he can make with a toy piano or a tin xylophone. If he's lucky enough to have parents who teach him to use his voice to explore pitch relations, he may catch on. Unfortunately, he can't make more than one sound at a time with his own voice, so he is disadvantaged compared to the budding architect who can combine his blocks into interesting structures all by himself, or the fledgling artist who can combine his shapes and colors without collaboration. Perhaps, with the development of synthesizers and electronic sound generation, some enterprising toy manufacturers will produce devices that will allow a youngster to explore pure pitch relationships all by himself. I was discussing this point with

my college theory class the other day and one young man remem–
bered that he first became aware of pitch relations by singing along
with the whine of his mother's vacuum cleaner. Now, there's a
hip kid!

"Does this mean," you may ask, "if one hasn't developed an
ear as a child, there is little hope of improvement as an adult?" I'm
glad you asked. The answer is an emphatic "no." It is simply a
matter of paying attention to some basic sound phenomena that can
be heard by anyone with normal hearing.

A few decades ago I was discussing this over lunch with a
colleague, and I stated that I suspected that there is no such thing
as a tone-deaf person (provided hearing was physically normal).
His response indicated that he considered me an ivory-tower
idealist, although he was gracious enough not to say it in so many
words.

That challenge was all I needed. I asked my department chair–
person to open a choral class for "non-singers." I convinced the
editor of the local paper to do a feature article about my idea, and I
began with a collection of curious, somewhat apprehensive, but
willing subjects. Well, we didn't perform the *St. Matthew Passion*
that semester, but we did get every singer to make the same
pitches at the same time. We even sang some simple four-part
music and only occasionally did someone fall out of the sound.

So what magic did we use to perform this miracle? None. The
miracle was performed eons ago when nature made ears that can
hear and recognize simple pitch relationships and vocal cords that
can reproduce these pitch relationships. All I did was point. All
they did was listen carefully to pitch relationships. They dis–
covered rather soon that they were on their way to becoming
musical people.

When I say "musical people" I'm not necessarily referring to those who read music, or who know that the key of A major has three sharps, or who took piano lessons for five years. I'm talking about people who can relate pitches in a musical way, whether or not they can name the pitches or write them down. My late brother Rodd was a musical person with incredible skills. I remember once lying on the sofa listening to him improvise on the piano for a couple of hours. We were in our early thirties, just a few years before he died. He never studied music formally. He just knew how to make it. Better than almost anyone. I sure do miss him.

It always bothered Rodd that he didn't read music proficiently. He did understand notation and earned a good living arranging and performing demos for songwriters. But he, like many other super talents I have known, could not bring himself to "start over" and study music formally. I guess, once you have reached adulthood, its pretty hard to stick to a regimen of musical ABC's, particularly when you have achieved a considerably high level of performance skills. You know, I think he probably read music better than he led us to believe. He may have manufactured a sort of personal-integrity camouflage to cover his lack of formal training.

Before we get back to work, let me tell you about one more memory I have of my brother. Rodd's girl friend Debbie also grew up around music. Her dad, my good friend Allan Davies, is a veteran studio singer and arranger and her mom is a piano teacher and a singer as well. Rodd, Debbie and I took my wife, Marlene, out to dinner to celebrate her birthday. We had decided on a popular seaside restaurant in Malibu, and there was a considerable wait for our table (even though we had a reservation) and we were there for probably three hours or so. During that time, there must have been six or eight performances of "Happy Birthday." Restaurant renderings of this traditional tune are usually not very memorable, from a musical standpoint at least, but these were particularly awful.

Rodd, Debbie and I decided that when it came time for Marlene to blow out the birthday candle, we would try to maintain some musical standards at our table. We agreed on a starting pitch, and decided who would sing melody and who would start on what note in the chord. When it was time, we improvised a three-part invention on "Happy Birthday" that old Johann Sebastian himself would have enjoyed. Although we were singing rather quietly (in contrast to earlier offerings), the noisy restaurant gradually became hushed. Then, at the final cadence of our little improvisation, the whole place exploded with applause.

So why was the Rodd-Debbie-Jerry trio so worthy of special attention? What did we know that the other performers that evening didn't? It wasn't extensive formal training, since I was the only one of the three who had a music degree. It wasn't ability to read music, since we didn't have any sheet music there. And even if we did, we probably couldn't have performed it without some rehearsal. What we three had was an awareness of and experience with the basic stuff of music -- pitch relationships. Not book-learning rules or "every good boy does fine." Simply the sounds themselves. All three of us had been listening to and playing with musical sounds since early childhood.

(Recently, we went to hear Debbie Davies headlining at B.B. King's new "blues" night club in Universal City. She's great!)

In contrast, I have known some experienced instrumentalists who could read fairly difficult music who had little musical idea of what they were playing. Although it might appear that they had grown up playing with musical sounds, they probably were not really listening. They had learned by association of notation directly to finger placement without paying attention to the organization of the sounds. They couldn't play by ear or impro–vise a simple harmonization of a folk tune. On the other hand, there are people, like Rodd, who can create incredible musical products, but who are not proficient music readers. Clearly, then, successful music making is not directly related to music reading ability.

Why, then, does music study consist largely of dealing with notation rather than with sounds? Every collegiate elementary music textbook I have ever seen deals principally with notation. Students who have some prior experience with sounds may be ready to learn some names and systems, but those who have not developed some sort of ear might as well be studying Martian. Since it is extremely boring to learn names for things you haven't experienced, the dropout rate is incredibly high. Those unmusical students who do succeed by sheer grit and determination are not necessarily any closer to finding musicality than the dropouts. Sadly, many of these pencil and paper musicians end up as teachers, who recycle the dry empty facts to the next generation of tin ears.

The math people came to grips with the "empty rules" problem and introduced "new math" a few decades ago. But music classes (even advanced ones) are still filled with students pushing notes around on a staff who have little idea what the sounds are that the notes represent.

To help alleviate the embarrassment of graduating music majors who can't hear, many college music programs include ear-training classes. Invariably, these classes have prerequisite theory classes that must be taken before one is admitted to them. Hey, folks! You got it backwards!

Remember when you learned about "doggies?" Your tutors were usually sharp enough to use the word only when there was a real doggie in sight, or a stuffed one, or at least a picture of one. Music teachers, on the other hand, have us memorizing nonsense symbols, hoping that at some future time our ear will mysteriously discover what the symbols represent. To be sure, it occasionally happens. But, isn't that doing it the hard way?

Lie #5: An interval is the distance between two pitches.

Truth: An interval is a qualitative perception of consonance.

In a music theory pencil and paper sense, an interval is indeed "the distance between two pitches," but in terms of human perception of sound it is not. Humans have a relatively poor sense of distance. Try holding your hands what you believe to be twenty seven inches apart and then have someone measure the distance with a yardstick. See what I mean? Now, without looking, click on a stop watch and then click it off in what you think is twenty four seconds. Before you look, how much will you wager on your accuracy? Get the idea? "Sure," you say, "but what does time and space have to do with musical intervals?"

Nothing! And that's the point. Humans don't perceive musical intervals as distances, they perceive them as vibrational ratios. That may sound a bit technical, but it really isn't. At least no more so than the previous discussion.

Let me illustrate. We identify colors as "green," "red," "purple," etc. You may know now that colors are really, in a physical sense, light frequencies. But, you *didn't* know it when you were a child learning your colors. You experienced different colors as *perceptual* experiences.

We experience pitch in a similar way. Even though pitch is really physically vibrating frequencies or speed, we hear pitches as "higher" or "lower." We translate a time and space physical hap-pening to a perceptual experience. We can't count the vibrations, but we can tell when they go faster (higher) or slower (lower). We can't tell the name of a given pitch with any precision (unless we are one of "them"), but we can tell when pitches are combined in certain ways.

In an earlier discussion, we noted that when we hear pitches combined in small-number ratios we are able to perceive these experiences as unique and identifiable. Also, that intervals having small-number ratios (1:2, 2:3, 3:4 etc.) are more consonant, and therefore are easier to hear and tune than the more dissonant intervals with high-number ratios (7:8, 8:9, etc.) We also showed that consonance/dissonance relationships are *qualitative* rather than *quantitative* perceptions.

If all of that still sounds a bit abstract, let me demonstrate. When intervals are inverted, they retain the same (or very similar) consonance/dissonance qualities. For example, when you move the bottom note of a fifth up an octave you get a fourth. Play these intervals on a keyboard (better yet, sing them) and you will hear that they sound very similar. (The invertable intervals are desig-nated here by the bold numbers on the keys.)

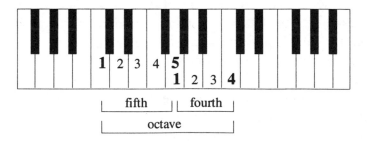

When you move the bottom note of a third up an octave you get a sixth. These, too, sound more like each other than like the fifth/fourth pair.

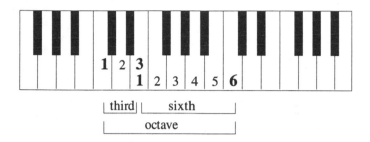

When you move the bottom note of a second up an octave you get a seventh, and (you guessed it) these intervals sound more like each other than like either the fourth/fifths or the third/sixths.

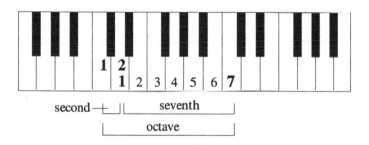

Notice that the difference in size varies from pair to pair. While the fourth/fifth pair are similar in distance, there is a great difference in size between the second and seventh. Also notice that, even though the distance of an octave is near the distance of a seventh, the sounds of the two intervals are very different. The seventh is far more dissonant than the octave.

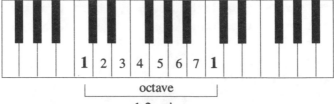

octave

1:2 ratio

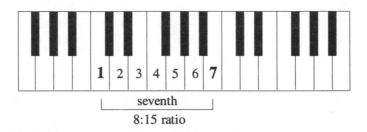

seventh

8:15 ratio

Clearly, it is the perceptual consonance/dissonance *quality* that makes these intervals similar and/or different from each other and contributes to their recognition. The similarity of their distance is *not* a significant factor in their recognition.

This being the case, it seems somewhat pointless to ask students to learn interval recognition by doing distance drills. I remember singing an exercise in college that went like this, on scale steps: 1-2-1, 1-3-1, 1-4-1, 1-5-1, 1-6-1, 1-7-1, 1-8-1. Now, I suppose if one did enough of this drill, the qualitative characteristics of each interval might be noticed. Thank goodness, some students learn in spite of poor teaching. Do you suppose that's where progress comes from?

**Lie #6: A scale is a series
of eight fixed pitches.**

**Truth: A scale is a system of many flexible
pitches whose tuning changes
slightly depending upon
harmonic context.**

I imagine your music teacher told you about scales and keys in pretty much the same way as mine. He said that a major scale is a one-octave pattern of whole and half steps in a specified order, and that the pitch you "start on" is the name of the key.

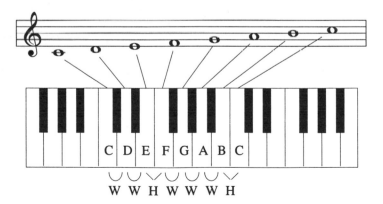

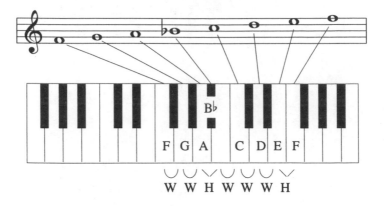

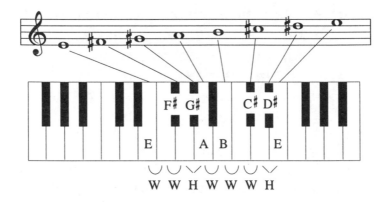

I can't swear that he actually said that a scale was one octave long, but I probably got that idea because all the scales we made in class (and in the textbook) were that long. I do know, however, that students still think this way because they show up in my music theory classes every semester with this naive concept firmly in place. For example, it never occurs to them that they can find scale step 6 by counting *down* from the keynote.

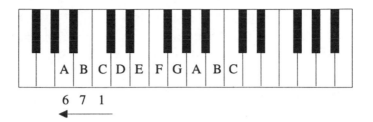

6 7 1

You probably have outgrown that silly idea by now, as I have, but do you ever catch yourself referring to the "starting note" or the "first note" of a scale? I think this phraseology is left over from the medieval idea of modes (scales with a fixed pattern of whole and half steps).

Medieval music theorists noticed, however, that some melo–dies were not contained between two keynotes an octave apart. When a chant covered the area from a fourth below the tonic pitch to a fifth above it, they added the prefix "hypo-" to whatever mode it was. In other words, they thought the mode needed a special name if the melody escaped the bounds of the one-octave scale from tonic to tonic.

DORIAN MODE

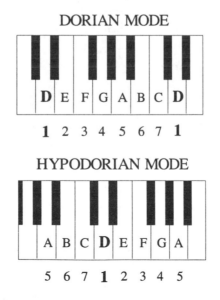

1 2 3 4 5 6 7 1

HYPODORIAN MODE

5 6 7 1 2 3 4 5

This practice seems to indicate that they did view music as being contained within an octave range. A modern application of this concept might be illustrated by observing how these two songs relate to a keynote.

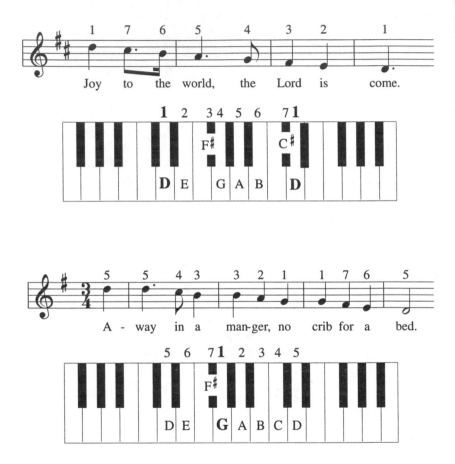

The first is contained between the high and low tonic note, while the second has the tonic near the middle of its range. These two tunes fit nicely into the range of one octave, but much music does not. So, our concept of what a key is should first of all be expanded to include the pitches outside a single octave. Second of all, a key isn't just a series of whole steps and half steps in a particular configuration. The early theorists thought it was because they were looking at music as if it were only a series of single pitches, one after the other (what we call *melody*). Even when composers started to combine two or more simultaneous lines of melody into polyphonic (many voiced) textures, theory was still locked on scales as the basis of musical organization. Oh, they knew of Pythagoras' description of intervalic harmonic relationships, and they made sure that their combined melodic lines intersected at strategic points with consonant intervals. They called that technique *counterpoint*, and we still do today.

During the Renaissance period, music became more and more polyphonic. It must have been great fun to sing all those intricately crafted musical tapestries. Near the end of the period it also became more chromatic. That is, composers added lots of sharps and flats to escape the boredom of the pure modal scales. What they eventually did, however, was to cause a musical revolution by the end of the sixteenth century toward a simpler musical product.

The Baroque period followed, during which composers discovered *chords*. Actually, musicians had previously begun to explore the idea of building musical structures vertically as well as horizontally, but hadn't develolped a systematic "how to." In the early eighteenth century, Phillipe Rameau described this new concept as *functional harmony*. What he said was that not only can melodic pitches be related to chords, but that chords can be related to *each other*.

When this information first reached me, it was still blurred by academic discussions of modes and scales, and something called "historical musical practice." I was encouraged to make harmonizations of dusty old chorale melodies, for which I had no particular fondness or familiarity, according to a set of rules handed down over the centuries. One curious rule was "thou shalt not make any voices move in parallel fifths or octaves." No one seemed to know why this musical practice was undesirable. I did notice that J. S. Bach didn't always subscribe to the idea, but somehow it was considered fashionable by the time I went to college.

I am now quite sure that the prohibition against parallel fifths and octaves had to do with the fact that, since these are very consonant intervals, voices moving parallel in this relationship would tend to lose their individual identity. So, why didn't my teachers say that? Didn't they know? Why didn't they ask? Or was this one of those pediatric rules like "Don't go into the street," after which we're supposed to grow up and find out the real truth for ourselves?

I want to believe that Rameau didn't have anything to do with the confusing way I was taught harmony. I plan to read his treatise some day (after I decide whether it's easier to learn French or to find the English translation) and find out for sure. In the mean–time, I'm satisfied that he was listening to the same harmonic relationships between pitches that we are, and that his physical world of sound was essentially the same as that which we perceive today. Most importantly, it was Rameau's idea of "functional harmony" that, for me, broke the case wide open. So let's talk about that.

First, let's look again at Pythagoras's string and see if it offers any further insights into the nature of a major scale. In the previous section we looked at the series of partials that occurs acoustically from a single pitch on C. It's on page 27, if you want to take a refresher peek. You may remember that the lower end of the series contains the pitches of the C major triad (C, E, and G). When we get up to the octave between partials 8 and 16 we get a few more pitches that appear to belong to the C major scale, as well as a few suspicious characters whose presence here seems a bit strange.

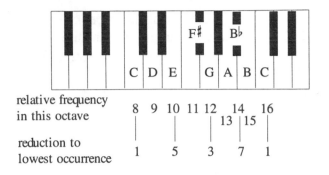

relative frequency in this octave			8	9	10	11	12	14	16
reduction to lowest occurrence								13	15	
			1		5		3		7		1

But, there is a bigger problem. There is no F, a very important in-gredient in the key of C. If you're beginning to suspect that there is more to the major scale than simply a stack of partials, you're right. There have been various scale theories proposed throughout the centuries, each offering a mathematical justification for the major scale. A *Pythagorean scale* was devised by piling up fifths and then reducing the resultant pitches to a single octave. It didn't come out even. Another system is called *just intonation*, which has some interesting relationships to Rameau's concept of chord relations, but it, too, has serious shortcomings. These and other attempts to explain the major/minor system mathematically have a common fatal flaw. They all appear to be based on the assumption that the scale is a collection of fixed pitches that relate directly to the tonic. Our ears tell us that this is not the case.

To me, the practical, as well as theoretical, solution is simply to realize that music should not be jammed into a rigid, inflexible system of fixed pitches. Tuning is a dynamic and lively process that is a natural part of the art of music. For example, scale step six tunes as the thirteenth partial only when the tonic note is the root. It tunes quite differently as the third of the subdominant root (scale step four). It changes again as the ninth of a dominant root (scale step five). You see, as the chords change, so does the tun-ing. If you want to try it, sing a high A while you switch back and forth from a C low note to an F low note. My ear hears the A slightly higher when the F is sounding. Now, try it with a G low note and see what happens.

This is the thing that really broke it open for me. As chords change, the tuning of the various scale steps change too. A repeated note is not necessarily a repeated *pitch*. How, then, does music hold together into a stable system? If accurate tuning is so flexible, what prevents the key center from wondering into the wild blue yonder? The answer has to do with Rameau's chord relations (although I don't think he talked much about flexible tuning.)

In our discussion of Pythagoras' string, we noted that the most consonant interval, other than the octave, is the fifth. If we use C as a central pitch, add the pitches a fifth higher and a fifth lower, then build major triads on each of these three pitches, we get all of the pitches of the C major scale.

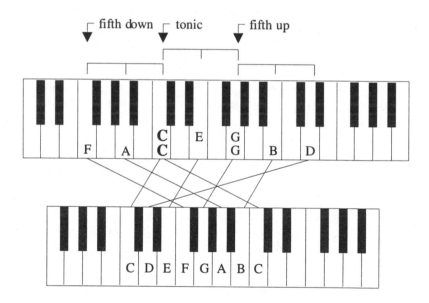

We have seen how the pitches E and G fit into the overtone series, or partials, of the pitch C to make what we call a major chord. Similarly, the G fundamental provides the tuning for B (4:5) and D (2:3), while the F fundamental provides the tuning for A (4:5) and C (2:3). Well, actually the C, since it is the *tonic*, or central pitch of the key, is really providing the tuning for the F, just as it provides the tuning for the G (2:3). Simplicity wins again.

We no longer need be concerned about the suspicious tuning of the A directly to the tonic C (13:16) since it can tune more fundamentally (4:5) to the F, its own "parent" pitch. It's the F that is directly responsible to be in tune with the C. Likewise, the B is not responsible to tune directly to the tonic (15:16) when its presence is sponsored by the G (4:5).

So, why did *none* of the many music teachers who contributed to my education tell me about this? Why did I have to *discover* what a major scale is all about almost by accident while thinking about and experimenting with tuning? The idea of deriving the scale from the three principle triads is *not* new. It was after I had put these ideas together for myself that I discovered my old friend Helmholtz had suggested this to be the case. (I wonder if television talk shows might have given him the exposure he needed to get his ideas out there.)

By means of the ratios of the pitch numbers already assigned for the consonant intervals, it is easy, by pursuing these intervals throughout, to calculate the ratios for the whole extent of the musical scale.

The major triad, or chord of three tones, consists of a major Third and a Fifth. Hence its ratios are:

$$C \ : \ E \ : \ G$$
$$1 \ : \ \frac{5}{4} \ : \ \frac{3}{2}$$
$$\text{or} \quad 4 \ : \ 5 \ : \ 6$$

If we associate with this triad that of its dominant G : B : D, and that of its sub-dominant F : A : C each of which has one tone in common with the triad of the tonic C : E : G, we obtain the complete series of tones for the major scale of C, with the following ratios of the pitch numbers:

C	:	D	:	E	:	F	:	G	:	A	:	B	:	C
1	:	$\frac{9}{8}$	:	$\frac{5}{4}$	:	$\frac{4}{3}$	:	$\frac{3}{2}$	:	$\frac{5}{3}$	:	$\frac{15}{8}$	:	2

[or   24 : 27 : 30 : 32 : 36 : 40 : 45 : 48]

Can you imagine how thrilled I was when I read that? Boy, I really love this guy!

Helmholtz did not really espouse flexible tuning. He, too, attempted to fuse his chord-derived scale steps into granite. Okay, so nobody's perfect. Somehow I think he would have arrived at a better conclusion if he had lived long enough.

So, what about those suspicious higher partials we were looking at earlier? Are they usable? Mozart didn't use many of them and might have said that the ones beyond 7 or 9 are not, but sensitive musicians since Debussy would probably want at least to include 11 and 13. Chord members corresponding to these upper partials serve to add color to musical sonorities, perhaps in a way related to how partials provide the characteristic colors of the various instruments.

In other words, I'm suggesting that effective tuning imitates the partials in Pythagoras's string rather exactly, and when a chord-full of pitches is produced in a manner approximating the tuning of partials, the result is that the individual pitches tend to disappear into the Gestalt of the sound itself. Like the Pierce Jazz Choir singing "into the chords."

Let's take a look and a listen. When pitches above the 6th partial are used, the resultant chord usually functions as a dom–inant (scale step 5), so a G root was selected for this illustration, thus placing the overall tonality on C. The numbers beside the notes on the staff and above the keyboard are the partials above G. The numbers below the staff are the scale steps of those pitches in the key of C.

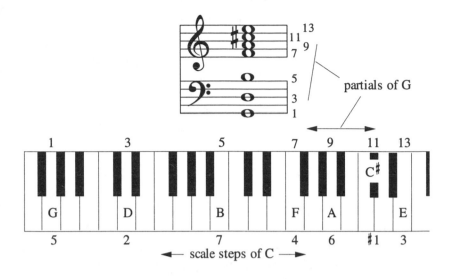

Of course, the keyboard can only approximate these pitches. The D is a tad higher than piano pitch, the B is usually sung higher, the F is considerably lower, the A a bit higher, the "C#" is not really very close to anything on the keyboard, and the E is perceptibly higher. I don't suppose you have a half dozen good string players handy, do you?

If the adjustments from piano pitch required to fine-tune basic triads are considered slight, the adjustments needed to tune the upper partials are enormous. While partials from 1 to 6 may be close enough to piano pitch to "recognize" them as those pitches, the 7th, 9th, 11th and 13th are definitely "in the cracks." So, does that make them unusable? I don't think so. Here's why.

In my vocal groups, the goal is to tune chords "until the notes disappear." We have found that when we all agree on vowel, resonance, brightness and other vocal variables, we can hear quite clearly where the pitch "should" go. When we move it there, our individual voices tend to disappear into the sonority. In other words, we are hearing the chord *quality* more than we are hearing the individual pitches.

I believe this happens because the pitches are relating to each other in the same way the partials in Pythagoras' string create timbre. We don't hear the individual overtones, or "little pitches," in the sound of a violin, or trumpet, playing a single note because they are perfectly "tuned" by nature. Similarly, to the extent that our tuning approaches "perfection," we tend not to hear the individual voices in a sonority. Have I done the research to prove this? No. It just makes sense to me. Newton experienced his falling apple; I experienced my "homogenized" chords.

In case you are getting the impression that I think I have it all figured out, let me assure you that I haven't. Every book needs a bit of mystery. Here's ours. The numbers indicate that the fifth partial (scale step 3) is lower than the tempered major third. Yet, I have observed that many pitch-sensitive musicians (particularly string players and singers) seem to prefer a tuning that is higher than the tempered third when the fifth of the chord is also sounding. Evidently, there is more happening here than just simple partials. Here's an opportunity for cutting-edge research.

In the meanwhile, the practical bottom line is that musical performers should approach tuning as a constantly changing process. Well-tuned major/minor music cannot be locked into a rigid "scale." That tends to make a performance wooden, lifeless, and ultimately boring. Aural sensitivity to flexible acoustic tuning breathes life and real excitement into a musical performance, and ultimately provides a more emotion-packed experience for both the performer and listener.

So, you see, a major scale is not just another mode like the medieval church scales. It, along with its alter ego, the minor mode, was a *new* idea developed by the intuitive musical artistry of late renaissance and early baroque composers and described by our clever friend, Phillipe Rameau. You're not convinced? You say you're not ready to give up on your "whole step--whole step--half step" routine? Just hang on. You haven't seen anything yet.

Lie #7: A key is the name of the first step of the scale.

Truth: A key is a system of harmonic relationships "revolving" around a central pitch.

The major/minor tonal system has some similarity to a solar system in that the tonic is somewhat like a sun, around which the other pitches revolve like satellites. If we chart the seven scale steps to show their harmonic relationship to the tonic pitch, we can learn something about their individual roles, or functions, in the major/minor system. Also, it will be helpful at this point to attach their functional titles, as well.

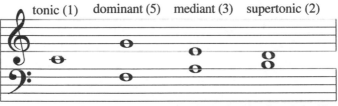

The dominant (a fifth above tonic) and subdominant (a fifth below it) are most closely related to the tonic harmonically (2:3), and serve to alternately pull the center of gravity away from the tonic. The mediants, presumably named because they are posi-tioned roughly halfway between the tonic and their respective dominants, are more distantly related harmonically to the tonic (4:5 and/or 5:6, depending on the mode). They are the "color" pitches, and supply the major and minor flavor to the music. (More about that soon.) The supertonic and leading tone are closest melodically to the tonic (a step above and a half step below) and, at the same time, are the most distant harmonically (8:9 and 15:16). It is these ironically combined characteristics in scale steps 2 and 7 that somehow work together to create the magnetism that pulls the music back toward the tonal center.

In my college theory book, these titles were listed in scale order.

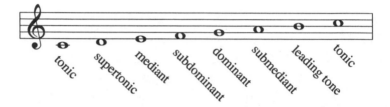

I got the idea that the subdominant was so named because it was "under" the dominant. I had no idea why the submediant was not under the mediant, however, but was actually three steps higher. But then, at that age you really didn't expect to know everything. If you picked up this idea from your teacher, you may now safely dispose of it. It's completely biodegradable and will dissolve naturally into that recyclable state where all discarded misconceptions go, ready to be used again by some future youthful music student.

The solar system analogy, like the one-octave scale, is fine for theoretical constructs, but like the traditional scale, should not be confined to one set of pitches. The "tonic" is not a single pitch, but is simultaneously all of the octaves relating to a selected pitch. Likewise, the dominant is also not a single pitch, and can be found at the same relative location between any two tonic pitches: a fifth above and a fourth below.

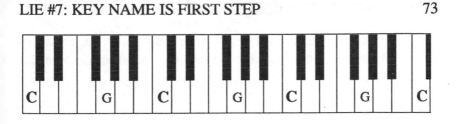

All the other "satellite" pitches in the key of C are standing by in their respective positions between any two tonics, waiting to go to work.

That may seem a bit overwhelming, but it really needn't be. There still are only seven primary "personalities" to deal with, even though they change their tuning according to who's in charge (something like people). All the octave doublings are simply clones. Each of the seven members is a kind of "abstraction" which is very distinctive and recognizable. Once they are seen and heard in their respective functional roles one should have little difficulty in learning to identify them.

To help my students begin this process, I developed a couple of learning aids. Here is a one-octave scale drawn with shapes that characterize the functions of the seven scale steps.

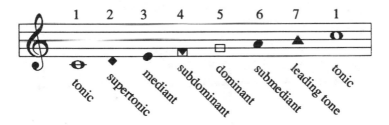

The tonic (1) is represented by a simple whole note, connoting a state of rest. The dominant (5) and subdominant (4) are represented by a rather strong symbol --a square "whole note" to differentiate it from the tonic. The mediant (3) and submediant (6) are black noteheads, suggesting that they are responsible for "coloring" (major and minor modes) the music. The supertonic is diamond shaped, pointing both up and down, suggesting that it wants to move up or down to a more restful scale step. The leading tone points upward, leaving no doubt about its tendency to release its restlessness by moving up to the tonic.

Scale step 4 not only has a square shape, denoting its role as the subdominant, but the square contains a triangle pointing downward suggesting that it has another role, as well. When appearing as the subdominant, scale step 4 has a tuning allegiance directly to the tonic.

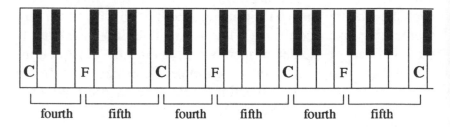

When the dominant chord (G root) is sounding, however, scale step 4 (F) changes its personality and becomes the 7th of that chord. Not only does its function change, but its tuning is vastly different. Remember that the 6:7 interval (fifth D to seventh F), is smaller than the 5:6 interval (third B to fifth D).

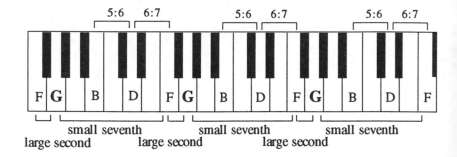

The difference in tuning is fairly easy to hear (assuming you are emancipated from tempered training). Play a C and sing the F above it. Move it around until you hear it lock. Now play the G below and slide your F down very slowly until you hear it in agreement with the G root. Yes, it is more dissonant than the C-F relationship, but it is just as clearly "in tune" when you slide it into focus.

In this graphic, scale step 4 is shown in both of these very different roles. The middle line is the tonic (no specific key). The note shapes are the same ones I showed you on the previous page. Here you can see how they function on the job. The numbers beside the notes are scale steps. The roman numbers below the notes indicate the scale step that is functioning as the root, or fundamental, for that chord. The number 7 by the V indicates that this is a four-note chord, containing a root, third, fifth and seventh.

| I | IV | V_7 |

There are a number of important things to notice in this graphic. First, note that the subdominant chord (IV) is an apparent mirror to the tonic chord (I). It actually is not a perfect mirror because the size of the thirds (from tonic up to mediant 3 and from tonic down to submediant 6) are not the same (check it on the keyboard). This pattern will become very interesting, however, when we look later at the relationship between major and minor mode.

Secondly, note that all of the "action" notes are in the dominant seventh chord (V^7). The magnetic dissonance in this chord is vividly clear. Scale step 7, in partnership with its harmonic ally, scale step 4, impels the music toward tonic harmony. Scale step 2, also having a restless nature, falls naturally toward tonic or, under some circumstances, moves up to scale step 3.

It may be helpful, at this point, to see what shows up when we translate the simple harmonic ratios that make up the major mode into real numbers representing vibrations per second. Let's arbitrarily pick 300 to represent tonic, then figure out what the vibrational ratios would be for the other scale members. The bold numbers to the left of the frequencies are the scale steps in the tonic and subdominant chords. The bold numbers on the right are the scale steps in the dominant seventh chord. (This graphic is essentially the same as the previous one except that it is expressed in numbers instead of notes.)

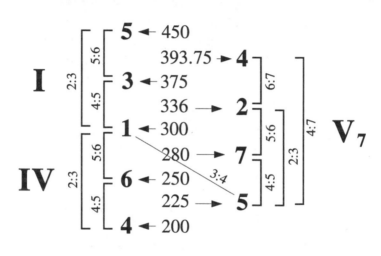

Notice the difference between scale step 4 in its subdominant tuning (200 up an octave would be 400) compared to scale step 4 in its role as seventh of the dominant chord (393.75). Significant? Definitely!

It might be argued that the major/minor system, including the distinctive characteristics of its scale steps, have been developed simply as a result of the musical practices of the past few centuries. Perhaps. But, I think there is good reason to believe that much of what was developed during that time was not so much invention as it was *discovery*. I think the idea of conceiving music in terms of harmonic relationships, as it was developed in the seventeenth century, was more a matter of becoming artistically aware of the physical properties of sound. Perhaps the impassioned love affair with tempered tuning, combined with the hardened crusts of traditional concepts of scales, has distracted us from these basic truths of nature. Perhaps if we take another listen to how poorly our choirs sing, and how difficult it is to train the ears of our young musicians, we will reconsider our unswerving devotion to tempered-tuned scales.

I hope it is clear now why singing mushy whole and half step scales is of little help in learning to hear harmonic relationships. It should also be clear why use of the keyboard as a standard for ear training does not yield much success. Musical tuning is a dynamic, constantly changing process, and a keyboard, with its fixed pitches simply can't do that.

I think singing related pitches against a sustained root is the best way to experience accurate tuning. In the discussion of pulse and meter later in this book, I will point out that physical movement seems to be vital to understanding rhythmic flow. It may also be true that physical involvement in producing well-tuned pitches is vital to perceiving harmonic relationships as well. If so, singing them is the easiest way for humans to physically make pitches, at least until we get more proficient at rubbing our hind legs together.

So, how far can human beings go in developing the ability to hear and produce these acoustical pitch relationships? While a perfect fifth and a major third are relatively easy to tune, it takes a bit more practice to tune a major second (whole step) and a minor second (half step). Whether or not it is possible to hear and reproduce the difference between an 8:9 whole step (scale steps 1-2) and a 9:10 whole step (scale steps 2-3) is a question that seems worth answering. Any post-graduate music students out there looking for a thesis?

I do know from practical experience, however, that when singers can be convinced to forsake their tempered-tuning habits and to really listen to the natural harmonic relationships between pitches, the result is quite astounding. Not only do chords "lock" so that the individual pitches tend to disappear into the sonority, but melodies also take on a fresh brilliance that a keyboard can only dream about.

Recently, the L.A. Jazz Choir was doing a sound check on stage before a performance at the Los Angeles Music Center. The orchestra had left for a break and we were running through a very challenging Earl Brown arrangement of *Midnight Sun*, an extremely chromatic composition (even before Earl added his own artistry). About two minutes into our *a cappella* rehearsal, Peter Matz, who was conducting that evening, walked onto the stage and, with a grin, played the last chord *with* the singers. They were right in the middle of the pitch. We grinned, too.

Sure, these are fine singers. But the point is that all of these singers have been experiencing "acoustic tuning" for a number of years now. One might think that "flexible" tuning would cause the tonality to waver, but we have found that just the opposite is true. Somehow, the sense of tonic prevails in the singers' memories, even though most of them do not have "pitch recognition."

So, what does all of this mean? Simply that, not only are tunes not carried in baskets, they are not carried in scales either, at least not in tempered-tuned scales. Humans have no apparent perceptual mechanism for conceptualizing the inner workings of a scale other than the harmonic relationships of its components. Those of us who did develop some accuracy in organizing the scale steps probably did so because we perceived (consciously or unconsciously) the physical truth of Pythagoras' string. If you doubt that statement, just witness the frustration of thousands of music students swimming around hopefully but helplessly in a morass of egg-shaped and tempered-tuned *do-re-mi*'s.

Lie #8: The minor mode is the aeolian mode inherited from the medieval church modes.

Truth: The minor mode is a "color" modification of the major mode.

It seems likely that our historical allegiance to scale theory prevented us from realizing how revolutionary Rameau's idea really was. Although the major scale bears no resemblance to any of the ancient church modes, the minor scale (specifically, the "natural" version of it) resembles the aeolian mode. This, evidently, suggested to theorists that they must be the same thing.

"NATURAL" MINOR SCALE IN C

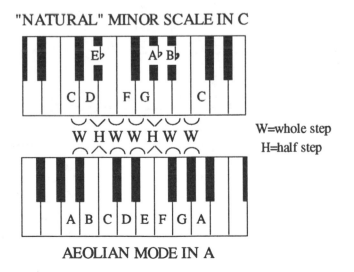

W=whole step
H=half step

AEOLIAN MODE IN A

Musical practice and acoustical facts would argue against such a view. The enormously important element in the musical break–through of the baroque composers was the discovery of the dominant seventh chord. We noted previously that it contains a unique harmonic mixture of active ingredients that impels the music toward a specific direction. The dominant seventh chord is the "motor" that makes the major/minor system happen.

any tonic -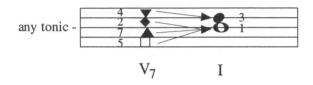

$$V_7 \qquad I$$

Baroque composers celebrated this new musical asset with a kaleidoscopic explosion of chromatic excitement. By arranging the specific intervals of the V7 chord, they could fling the tonal direction toward any destination that suited their musical fancy.

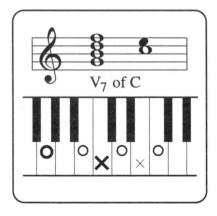

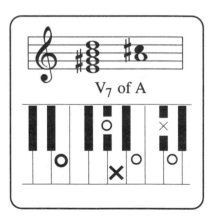

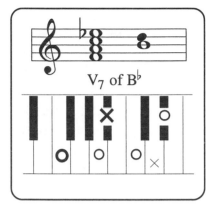

V_7 of B♭

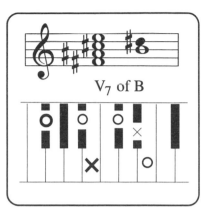

V_7 of B

What is it that makes this chord so unique and powerful? Just the most fascinating and mysterious little interval in all of tonal music--that's what! The medieval and gothic composers didn't know what to do with it, so they avoided it and called it *musicus diabolicus*, or "the devil of music." The Renaissance composers, being more worldly wise and daring, toyed around with it, but not without some caution and perhaps a touch of guilt. They attempted to "correct this flaw" in music's nature, and apologetically called the results *musica ficta*, or "false music." The informal name of this energetic little trouble maker is the tritone (so named because it consists of two pitches that are three whole steps apart on the keyboard). It is unique in that it is the only fifth in the major mode that is not "perfect," or in other words, does not have a 2:3 ratio.

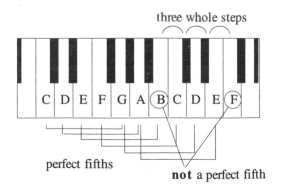

The other side of this coin is that, because there is only one tritone per key, any given tritone belongs only to one key (but be careful, spelling and tuning counts). Look at this. The tritone F♯-C belongs only to the key of G. It's the only major scale that has both an F♯ (scale step 7) and a C (scale step 4). Its subdominant neighbor, C major, has no sharps or flats, and therefore, an F natural. Its dominant neighbor, D major has two sharps, one of which is C♯. (If we extended this relational pattern to all of the other major keys farther away, we would find that none has this specific tritone unique to the key of G.)

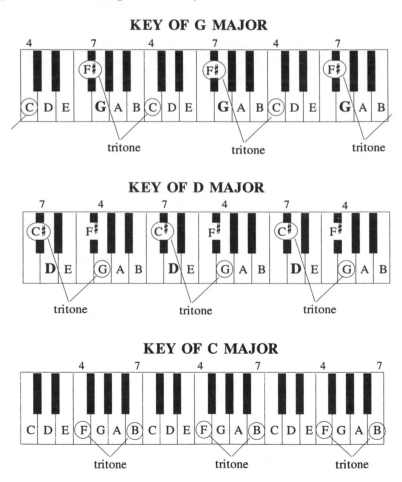

If we take the F♯-C tritone in the Key of G, and respell it as G♭-C (the same two notes on the keyboard), it now belongs to the key of D♭, the only major key that has both a G♭ (scale step 4) and a C (scale step 7). Of course the tuning changes when the sounds are produced by flexible means.

KEY OF D MAJOR

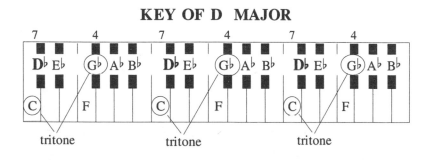

Would you enjoy a little "ooh, wow!"? Notice that the dominant roots of these two sound-alike tritones are also a tritone apart. I don't think the baroque composers took much advantage of this little gem of information, but progressive jazz musicians in our own century found out that you can substitute one for the other with a very "cool" effect.

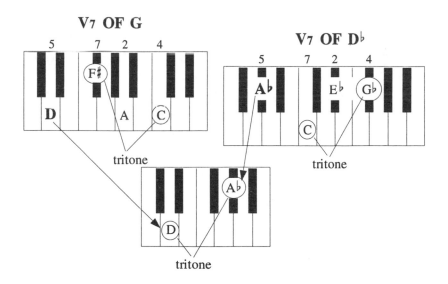

The dominant functional tritone always and only occurs on scale steps 4 and 7. Or 7 and 4, if you prefer. You see, it's the same size (in terms of tempered tuning keyboard intervals) even when you invert it (turn it upside down). It's the same distance (three whole steps) from B up to F as it is from B down to F. Another "ooh, wow!"

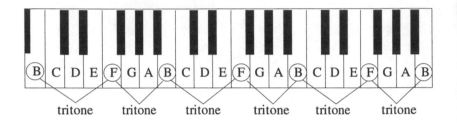

How about one more? The tonic of the key of C major, having no sharps and flats, is a tritone away from the tonic of F♯ major, having *six sharps*, as well as from F♯'s sound-alike, G♭ major, which has *six flats*. A difference of six sharps or flats is the most possible, making C and F♯ as far away from each other as possible, both harmonically and melodically (*six* half steps). Ooh, wow!

Yes, there are keys of seven sharps (C♯ major) and seven flats (C♭ major), but they don't count because on the keyboard they sound like D♭ major (five flats) and B major (five sharps) respectively, making them *closer* to C major. Besides, both of these are only a half step away from C melodically. (Another little "ooh, wow!")

When you first get into the symmetrical design of the major/minor system, you're almost transported into a mystical reverence for musical numbers. Upon closer inspection, however, you begin to see that it is all very logical and no more mysterious than the inner workings of this computer I'm pounding on. Hmmmm. On second thought.........

Speaking of mysterious, please don't forget that all of these keyboard enharmonic (spelling) transformations will be slightly "morphed" as they slide into various tonalities. Well-trained ears will tend to hear them in one key or another. Its something like those optical illusions we used to see in the funny papers where a geometric figure first appears to be seen one way and then another. Even when played on a keyboard, our perceptions takes the "reality" and transforms it into an "experience." One person's E-B♭ can be another persons E-A♯. And one person can learn to phase them back and forth at will.

So, this wild and unruly creature called the tritone was finally tamed and put to work, doing the bidding of countless music makers, from the palaces of seventeenth century Venice to the twentieth century streets of New York's Tin Pan Alley. Com—posers used this device, in combination with a dominant root, to send the music to any tonality they wished.

Now, here is the kicker. The dominant seventh chord is an essential part of *both* major and minor music. Also, there is no dominant seventh chord in the aeolian mode. When you spell a seventh chord on the fifth step of the aeolean scale you don't find a tritone. No tritone--no action.

AEOLIAN MODE IN A

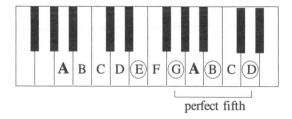

perfect fifth

What, then, is the logical (and acoustical) basis for the minor mode, if not the aeolian scale? Actually, its pretty simple. Watch what happens when you slide the third of a major triad down to the next "locked in" position. The large third (4:5) now occurs between the third and fifth and the small third (5:6) is now between the root and the third. This simple move transforms the major triad into the minor triad.

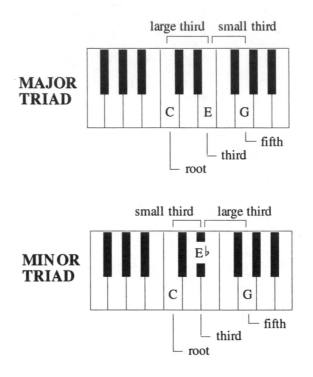

Logically, these two configurations of a perfect fifth, a large third, and a small third are the ONLY ONES POSSIBLE. I suppose that's so obvious that you are wondering why I brought it up. Well, for two reasons. One is that my teacher threw these triads in with the diminished triad and augmented triad as if they were just another way to make chords. I think that blurs their importance in understanding how music works. The other reason is that it demonstrates that the major/minor concept appears to be a logically *closed system* (at least, in terms of its basic structure). In other words, it contains relationships that are symmetrically balanced and its parts interact with all of its other parts in a logical and organized way. Does that take all the mystery out of it? Not at all. Often, when I discuss these matters with a class of neophyte theorists, I think I learn more than they do about the fascinating patterns and possibilities of this incredible gift of nature.

All right. Enough goose pimples. Let's get back to work.

The difference between major mode and minor mode is simply the positioning of scale steps 3 and 6. My teacher called these the *modal degrees* of the scale. This was one of the good things he told me. It was the beginning of my understanding that scale steps had special jobs to do. This is how it works. If we take the chords function chart from the previous discussion, and make the I and IV chords minor instead of major, we have the minor mode.

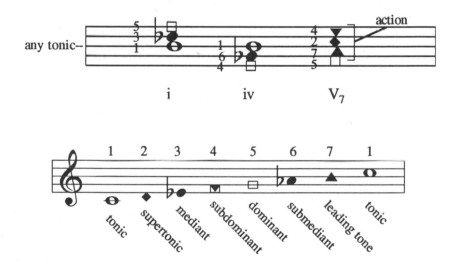

Yes, it's that simple. We don't want to modify the V7 chord or we lose the tritone. If we lose the tritone we lose the action and end up back in the middle ages with an aeolian scale.

What makes it *not* so simple is the convolutions we go through to write the music in terms of our traditional system of key signatures. But, we'll deal with that later.

To wrap this up, the major/minor system is a dual-faceted phenomenon, like white/black, yes/no, in/out, left/right, etc. If not outright opposites, at least major and minor modes are complementary alternatives coexisting in a unique and wonderful organization of musical perception. Now, what medieval mode can make that claim?

Lie #9: There are three minor scales: natural, harmonic and melodic.

Truth: Chromatic adjustments can be made in the minor mode, according to harmonic context, to accommodate the step-and-a-half between scale steps ♭6 and 7.

As I remember, it was this business of the three different minor scales that caused my initial suspicion that my music teachers may not have it all together. Like most conscientious music students, I had been pounding away on my natural, harmonic and melodic scales until they slid off my fingers like water on waxed paper. I could hardly wait to find some music that actually used these melodic configurations. I did find considerable melodies that appeared to use the "natural" minor scale pattern. This was not surprising, I thought, because it was identical to the aeolian mode.

"NATURAL" MINOR SCALE IN C

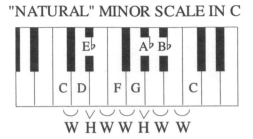

W H W W H W W

I found a significant number of melodies using what appeared to be the "melodic" form. This was the one where you raised scale steps 6 and 7 on the way up and lowered them (restored them to their "natural" position) on the way down.

"MELODIC" MINOR SCALE IN C

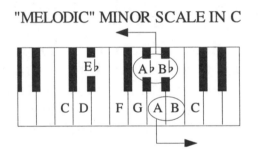

But, frequently I found *descending* melodies with a raised 7-6. Well, I knew the treatment for rules that didn't seem to work. You simply said that "rules were made to be broken," and that made everything right. But, it really didn't. This exception happened frequently enough to raise my suspicion that this rule needed more than an apologetic "excuse me, but..." It needed a basic overhaul.

Rarely did I find a melody that used the "harmonic" pattern. Upon inquiry, I was told that the harmonic minor scale applied more to harmony than it did to melody. That made some sense, because it had this big melodic gap in it.

"HARMONIC" MINOR SCALE IN C

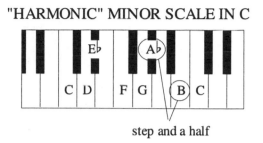

step and a half

But, if it was mainly for harmony, why was I busting my fin-gers in daily practice to learn to play it melodically? Something was definitely weird here. It's not having spent all that practice on something that was not very practical that bothers me. It was that my teacher didn't seem to know what was going on that got me to thinking about all of this.

Well, here we are about three decades later. As you know, I *have* been thinking about all of this. So, here's what I think.

First of all, we can knock off the daily drilling of harmonic minor scales. Secondly, we can quit lying about "raising on the way up" and "lowering on the way down." Thirdly, we can take another look at this whole business of "minor scales."

Okay, let's go. In the *major* scale, as we noted earlier, all the steps are either whole steps or half steps, allowing for nice graceful melodic motion. When we use minor chords on tonic and subdominant, scale steps 3 and 6 are lowered. This causes no melodic problem near scale step 3, where it simply moves the half step from 3-4 to 2-b3 and, reciprocally, the whole step from 2-3 to b3-4. However, lowering scale step 6 not only makes a half step between 5 and b6, it creates a step-and-a-half between b6 and 7, putting a sort of pothole in the melodic road.

(Please understand that this discussion has nothing to do with the charming ethnic steps-and-a-half in Slavic and gypsy music. Those intervals are there on purpose. We are talking here about minor scales as employed in the mainstream of European art music.)

Repairing the melodic surface between ♭6 and 7 is very easily accomplished, however. Composers did it with ease. It was the music theorists, with their silly scales who created the confusion. The solution is as simple as a passing tone. The choice of *which* passing tone is a matter of *harmonic context*.

When dominant harmony is sounding, the leading tone (scale step 7) is essential but the lowered submediant (♭6) is not. Therefore, melodies moving through this area will use a "raised" submediant (natural 6) as a passing tone between 5 and 7, eliminating the step-and-a-half gap. And IT DOESN'T MATTER WHETHER THE MELODY IS GOING UP OR DOWN.

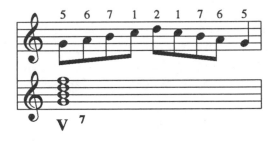

When tonic or subdominant harmony is sounding, the leading tone is not essential but the minor flavor *is*. So melodies moving through this area can use a lowered scale step 7 (called a subtonic instead of a leading tone under these circumstances) as a passing tone between ♭6 and tonic. Pothole fixed. Again, IT DOESN'T MATTER WHICH WAY THE MELODY IS GOING.

i

iv

To illustrate how this works in practical music, here is a simple tune in the major mode.

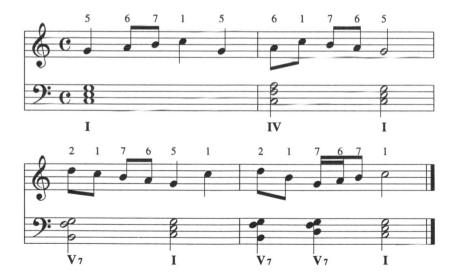

Now, here is the same tune in the minor mode. Notice which steps require modification and under what harmonic circum–stances.

So, why do we need three carved-in-granite scales to explain this simple procedure? Actually, as you know, I'm not that crazy about scales in general. But then, we should consider that I may be in a state of overreaction. So, how's this? I would be pleased if you will be kind enough to join me in a bit of suspicion regarding the matter of three minor scales. Thank you very much.

Lie #10: The key signature of a minor key is the same as that of its relative major.

Truth: The traditional minor key signature has one more flat (or one less sharp) than it really needs.

A key signature is a handy thing. It collects all the flats or sharps you are normally going to use in a piece of music and puts them at the beginning. You simply remember which ones they are and adjust those pitches appropriately whenever they show up. No need to write them in every time. This works great in the major mode. Whenever you see an accidental (a sharp, flat or cancel sign) in the music, you know that note doesn't belong to the prevailing tonality. The melody below is in the key of B♭. The raised scale step four (E natural on the second syllable of "early") shows that the tonality has temporarily moved to the key of F, which has a B♭ but not an E♭.

Oh— say can you see by the dawn's ear - ly light

A key signature doesn't tell you for sure what the tonality is, however, since different modes use the same signatures for different tonics. A signature having two flats usually indicates either Bb major or G minor, but it could be C dorian. You have to look at the way the music is put together in order to tell. In the example above, the F-D-Bb opening melodic pitches argue for Bb major. (Isn't there a better way?)

In the minor mode, however, accidentals in the music don't necessarily mean that you have left the home key. Minor-mode music has "raised" 7th scale steps all over it. It makes it look like that note doesn't belong to the prevailing tonality--but it does. This melody is entirely in the key of C minor.

(There must be a better way.)

We don't really have a system of key signatures that fits the minor mode. Instead, we borrow the major signature that is most like whatever minor scale we want to accommodate. For example, C minor, having a lowered mediant and submediant, has an Eb and an Ab.

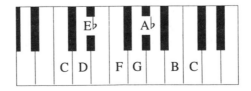

The most similar major scale is E♭: having a B♭, E♭ and A♭.

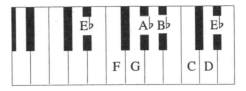

Its signature shows 3 flats:

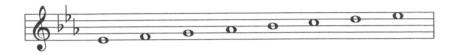

We don't want the B♭ (except when we use it as a passing tone to fix the melodic pothole). It really isn't a natural-born member of the key of C minor because the dominant seventh chord, which *is* a blood relative, has and *needs* a B natural leading tone in order to do its job. Without the B natural, we're right back in the Middle Ages with the aeolian mode. No thanks!

Tradition uses the three-flat signature and cancels the B♭ in the music where needed.

What a drag! How about this signature for C minor.

It shows the scale members of the *real* "natural" minor. And no accidental is needed for scale step 7.

So, here are our options:

1) We can devise a whole new set of signatures for minor keys. Then we would know right up front whether a key signature was indicating a major or minor key. We would then present *two* sets of key signatures for our freshmen music students to memorize. On second thought, this doesn't really appeal to me much.

2) We can live with the present system. I guess it doesn't make much sense to fight City Hall unless you have a decent chance of winning. At my age, I've learned to live with quite a number of imperfect systems--government... marriage... my golf swing.... I'm sure I can manage one more.

(Okay, so there *is* a better way, but it probably isn't practical to pursue it.)

So, dear colleague, a favor. Please inform your students that *relative minor* and *relative major* refers to the reciprocal relationship between a major and a minor key who share the same key signature, but *not* the exact same scale steps. And likewise, please inform them that *parallel minor* and *parallel major* refers to minor and major keys who share the same tonality, as well as all the same scale steps *except 3 and 6*. Thanks.

Lie #11: The first two notes of *My Bonnie Lies Over the Ocean* is a good sound model for the major sixth on scale steps 1 to 6.

Truth: The first two notes of *My Bonnie* do not occur on scale steps 1 and 6.

I am a firm believer in the value of sound models, or crutches, as they are sometimes called, for training the ears of student mu-sicians. Identification of on-the-job constructs is the best way to learn about how music works and to attach labels. "Oh, say can you see" is a very well-known phrase containing the members of the tonic triad.

"Three blind mice" can help a student to hear scale steps 3-2-1. And the famous "Here comes the bride" is the all-time favorite for the ascending perfect fourth, although I have frequently heard "For auld acquaintance" doing the same job.

A problem arises, however, when a concept label is attached to the wrong job. The major sixth that opens the melody of *My Bonnie* is the interval from scale steps 5 up to 3.

I constantly see this tune being used as a sound model for the major sixth, even in textbooks, *without* the information that it does not use scale steps 1 to 6. The tonic in this melody falls on the word "lies," not on the first word, "My." It has become a crusade with me to stamp out this debilitating teaching practice. I make it a point when appropriate (for example during the audition of a singer for the L.A. Jazz Choir) to ask what the scale steps are in the opening of *My Bonnie*, and almost without exception the answer is, "Oh that's a major sixth. One, six." And these are EDUCATED MUSICIANS.

I think this "lie" is a byproduct of thinking in terms of a "first" note of the scale. It suggests that melodies start on the tonic note, a naive idea that stubbornly persists. It came up in my beginning theory class the other day. Sadly, it persists in the viscera of many music teachers who know that many melodies don't start on tonic, but who nevertheless continue to suggest to students that the phrase "here comes the bride" is an example of scale steps 1-4 instead of 5-1.

These are probably the same teachers who never outgrew the concept that "all intervals are measured up from tonic." For those of you who didn't get this far in your theory lessons, let me give you the background.

We were taught "if the upper note of an interval is in the major key of the lower note, the interval is major or perfect; major, if it's a 2nd, 3rd, 6th or 7th; perfect if it is a 4th or 5th." No problem!

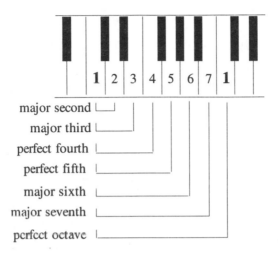

To continue, "a minor interval is a half step smaller than a major one, a diminished interval is a half step smaller than a minor or perfect one, and an augmented interval is a half step larger than a major or perfect one." Again, this is a logical and correct way to figure out (notationally) the size of every interval in music.

But, what it doesn't do is demonstrate how intervals work together in a key, and, more importantly, what they sound like while at work. What's worse, it suggests that the bottom note of an interval is always the tonic.

Paul Hindemith, the well-known twentieth century composer, presented a very logical and practical theory of intervals in his book *The Craft of Musical Composition*. He shows the perfect fifth with its root on the bottom, and its inversion, the perfect fourth, with its root on top. He treats the rest of the intervals in a similar manner. His view of intervals makes perfect sense, both in terms of acoustic as well as practical music making. Unfortunately, his ideas never made the trip from graduate seminars to the rank and file thinking of music teachers. Too bad! So, in honor of Mr. Hindemith, let's take a look at intervals as they per– form their functions in the major/minor system.

Let's see what intervals appear where in the tonic triad.

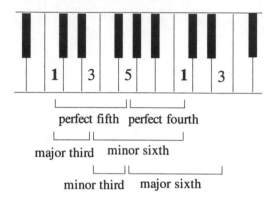

Now we can see the major 6th in *My Bonnie* (scale steps 5-3) and the perfect 4th of "here comes" (5-1) in their proper tonal context, and what's more we can *hear* them in that context. Of course, melodies are harmonized by more chords than tonic, so let's look at the intervals contained in the other two principle chords in the major mode. First, the subdominant chord (IV):

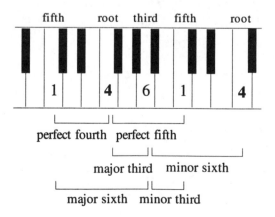

Since this is simply another major triad, all of the same intervals are here. They just appear in different places in the scale.

Now, the dominant seventh chord (V7):

Many more intervals here. The same ones that occurred in the tonic and subdominant triads are here as well, but with the addition of the chord 7th (scale step 4) we get the "blue" sounding 7th and 2nd, a smaller minor 3rd and larger major 6th, as well as the two tritones. I want to talk more about these additional inter-vals, but let's stay with the simpler ones a bit longer.

I think our sense of tonic plays a major part in identifying intervals at work. For example, the 3-5 (we're talking scale steps here) minor third sounds a bit different to me than the 6-1 minor third. I hear the former sounding in the context of the tonic triad and the latter sounding in the context of the subdominant triad. Sure, both triads are major chords and both of these minor thirds are functioning as 3rd-5th of their respective harmonies. But, to me, the influence of the tonic as the fifth of the subdominant supplies a significant difference in flavor. Play and sing. What do you think?

The 6-1 minor third can also be tuned as a 13:16 ratio, as in the context of a tonic root, but this relationship is probably too obscure to be perceived by a beginner. The 6-1 minor third is much easier to hear in the context of subdominant harmony in its simpler 5:6 ratio. When A and C are sounded without context, there is a very strong tendency, even by novices, to imagine an F root. One would suspect that this is caused by the acoustical simplicity of a major triad, in which 5:6 is the ratio between the third and fifth of that chord. This phenomenon is sometimes referred to as hearing the *combination tone*.

The 1-♭3 minor third is probably perceived in quite a different way than the 3-5 minor third. Even though the acoustical ratio is probably 5:6 in both cases, the influence of the sense of root created by the presence of the "fifth" as well as the flavor of the minor triad as a whole makes these two minor thirds sound quite different.

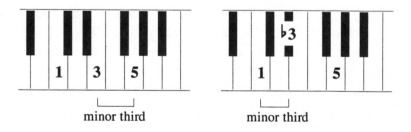

minor third   minor third

A great training drill for somewhat advanced ears is to play a minor third and alternately shift the focus from 3-5 to 1-♭3 by imagining the "missing" pitch that would complete the chord. For example, play E and G while imagining C (C major chord), then imagining B (E minor chord). The tuning may not change, but the "flavor" sure does.

Let's get back to intervals measured up from tonic. If a minor second is thought of as "a half step smaller than a major second," then it follows (in the mind of a student) to express it as 1-♭2. Now, what does ♭2 have to do with a major or minor key? Nothing!

Doesn't it make more practical sense to systematize basic interval theory in the context of the system itself? We know that major intervals occur from tonic up to scale steps 2, 3, 6, and 7. Did you ever notice that minor intervals occur on those same scale steps when measured *down* from tonic? Instead of "adjusting" for minor intervals, we have a system that identifies them *within* the context of the major mode.

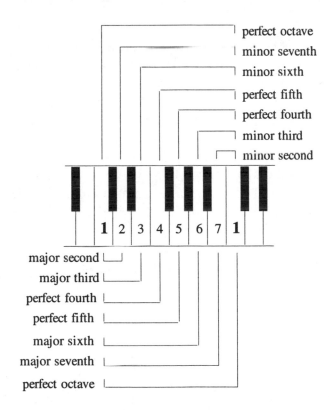

No one ever pointed that out to me. I just noticed it one quiet afternoon when I had nothing better to do than think about intervals. I'm sure I'm not the first to see this, but I've never seen it in a music theory book. Have you?

We don't have to change all of our "interval identification" test questions. We simply teach students to notice which note is in the key of the other.

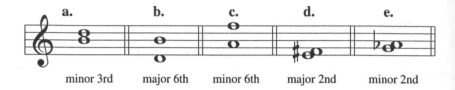

Item a. - The lower note, B, is in the key of the upper note D, therefore this is a minor third. Another way is to try a third as 1-3 and as 6-1 and see which one works. (Also, note that an exper-ienced musician can see this interval as the upper third of a G major triad, where it falls naturally in the overtone series, and identify the interval that way.)

Item b. - The upper note (B) is in the key of the lower note (D), and therefore a major sixth. (Again, an experienced musician can see this interval as 5-3 in the key of G. Remember *My Bonnie*?)

Item c. - The lower note (A) is step 3 of the upper note (F).

Item d. - The upper note (F♯) is step 2 of the lower note (E).

Item e. - G is the leading tone of A♭.

Perfect fourths and fifths are easily identified because both notes are in each other's keys. That's why they're "perfect." Did your teacher ever tell you that? Mine didn't.

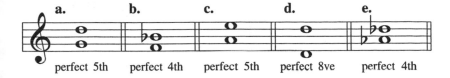

Item a. - G is in the key of D, and D is in the key of G.

Item b. - F is in the key of B♭, and B♭ is in the key of F.

Items c. through e. - Ditto

Diminished and augmented intervals can be handled in the traditional manner, by comparing them to the nearest major, minor, or perfect interval.

Item a. - There is a C in the key of A♭; C♯ makes the interval a half step larger, therefore augmented. Or, there is a C♯ in the key of A; A♭ makes the interval a half-step larger, therefore augmented.

Item b. - There is a B in the key of E, therefore this is diminished. (An experienced musician immediately sees this as 7-4 in the key of F. Remember, the E-B♭ occurs as a functional tritone only as 7-4 in the key of F major.)

Item c. - F up to E♭ would be minor; F♯ makes it smaller, therefore diminished. Or, F♯ up to E would be minor; E♭ makes it smaller, therefore diminished.

Item d. - The only white-note augmented fourth. (Either a B♭ or an F♯ would make it perfect.)

Item e. - Yes, E♯, not F. I thought I would mention this in case you didn't know that white notes can be sharps or flats. If you spelled it G-F it would be a minor seventh, not an augmented sixth. Again, spelling counts.

I hope your teacher didn't have you identifying intervals by counting half steps! What a time consuming, misleading, and ultimately useless teaching practice. This is even more disturbing than the "every good boy does fine" technique of teaching lines and spaces. Perhaps the latter might be justified for teaching young children, just to get them started (although I doubt it). But *neither* should be used by adults. It simply postpones learning the real concepts and only serves to slow down fast thinking. Please try to discard any residual tendencies you may have that tempt you to think this way. I suspect that these plastic concepts may not be biodegradable and may very well continue to exist somewhere in the thinking of the once-infected, just itching to be used. I don't know how many half steps there are in a perfect fifth, and I don't ever want to know.

Let's get back now to the additional intervals that occur in the dominant seventh chord. Since it is basically a major chord, it has the 4:5 major third, the 5:6 minor third and the 2:3 perfect fifth and their inversions. But with the addition of that next higher "out of tune" partial, it contains the 4:7 "minor 7th" (and its inversion, the 7:8 "major" 2nd), the 6:7 "minor 3rd" (and 7:12 "minor" 6th) and the wild and woolly 5:7 (and 7:10) tritone.

Here, the difference between tempered and acoustic tuning is too significant to toss off as "not perceptible." It is an outright irresponsible teaching practice to imply that the "tritone" between scale steps 1 and ♯4 is the same interval as between 7 and 4. When the melodic tritone appears in its natural habitat, as 4-7 or 7-4, it is normally functioning and tuning as some kind of dominant harmony. When it appears elsewhere, it should be understood to have some other purpose. Its tuning will depend on its harmonic context, and will not be heard (or conceived) as the functional dominant harmony tritone.

I'm amused when I hear a teacher of ear training lamenting that he can't find many good sound-model melodies that start out with a tritone. The reason he can't find them is because melodies seldom start with a functional 7-4 or 4-7 tritone. They more frequently start with pitches that establish tonic harmony (even when dominant harmony is used as a "pickup" chord). I'm not amused, however, when I see a sound model for the tritone that begins with a skip from scale steps 1 to #4.

Ma - ri- a.___ I   just kissed a girl named Ma - ri- a.___

The supporting harmonic background for the opening of this phrase is a tonic chord, therefore the structural melodic interval here is the perfect 5th, 1-5. The #4 is simply a chromatic appoggiatura (a type of non-chord tone) that relates to 5. *Maria* serves absolutely no purpose as a sound model for a functional tritone. In fact, if presented as an example of a tritone, this melody is actually "lying" to the student. A functional tritone doesn't sound like this. More specifically, it doesn't tune like this.

Under some circumstances, even the melodic scale steps 4-7 might *not* be a dominant 5:7 or 7:10 tritone.

Here, the 4-7 melodic interval is not a functional tritone. The 7 is simply an embellishment to 1 (it happens four times here), while 4 is performing a *subdominant* function in a chromatic scalewise line which continues upward to #4, 5, #5 etc. The underlying harmony at that point is a ii7 chord, a subdominant family member. If you're going to use sound models to learn interval recognition, make sure that the model represents the concept.

Does it really matter that a "theoretical" difference exists in some of these intervals? Are these differences really important in the perception and performance of music? By now you know my position on these questions, so I won't bore you with additional arguments. You simply will have to experiment for yourself and see whether or not "acoustic tuning" puts a new sparkle in your musical performance and clarity in your perceptions. I know it will. I've been there.

Here's a drill that I have used successfully with my students. Pick a key. Locate the appropriate tonic, dominant and sub-dominant roots on a keyboard (preferably a sustaining one, like an organ or synthesizer). As you play a root, sing the chord tones on that root. When you shift to another root, sing those chord tones skipping from one to the other. Go slowly, sing with a straight vibratoless tone, and listen carefully to the acoustical relationship between your voice and the keyboard. When you are comfortable with this drill, sing the passing tones between the chord members. When you feel like a real expert, sing a pitch and change to dif-ferent roots and see if you hear any difference in tuning. If so, you're "in there."

Lie #12: The major scale is one of a number of scales (or modes) that have been used by composers throughout history.

Truth: The major/minor system is the most unique, practical, exciting, and natural musical construct that has been devised in the history of music.

If that "truth" sounds a bit like a "big finish" to you, you're perception is right. We'll use this discussion as a sort of summary of the preceding ideas and pull them together into an overall perspective.

The major/minor system is not just another scale. It fits right into Pythagoras' description of how pitches naturally and perceptually relate to each other. It is a logical extension of his discussion of "partials" and "overtones." It solves the mystery of the *tritone*, the diminished fifth that early church composers dubbed *musicus diabolicus*. It demonstrates that harmonic roots, as well as single pitches, have natural acoustical relationships within a tonal system. To think of the major/minor system as just another scale is to miss its whole import in the process of discovering musical truth.

When this new musical system was presented to the world, it should have enhanced and expanded skills in acoustic tuning. Instead, it became the major cause of acoustical neglect. The exciting thing about the major/minor system was that it explained how to modulate freely to any other key. Composers went wild with this new toy. But there was one big problem. While the strings, winds, and singers had no trouble adjusting their tuning in

distantly related keys, the keyboards couldn't do it. Their mech-
anical pitches were locked into whatever key they were tuned to.
There were some keyboards built with extra strings tuned to
closely related keys, but the whole thing became too cumbersome.
Then came the big breakthrough--tempered tuning! Bach was so
excited about it he composed two books of preludes and fugues in
every key, entitled The *Well-Tempered Clavier*.

It appears that musical minds since that time have been distracted from Pythagorean theory because of this great new system
of tuning. I guess it became old fashioned and anti-progressive to
talk about the natural acoustics of sound. Man had invented
something "better."

It would seem that the brilliant harmonies of Wagner, Tchai-
kovsky, Debussy and other nineteenth century Romantics would
have revived an appreciation for pure acoustical tuning. Our
quotes earlier from Helmholtz indicate that it didn't happen. But,
by the time we get to the twentieth century, we see a *conscious*
intent to negate tonality by Schoenberg and his disciples. I suppose, given the fact that you have an instrument that is already
doing a good job of obliterating human tonal sensitivities, you
might as well finish the job by writing music for it.

Interestingly, Hindemith never bought the idea of atonal
music. Like Bach, he composed a set of keyboard pieces in every
key, called *Ludus Tonalis*, but constructed them in a neo-classical
manner of clarity, balance and harmonic relationships.

By the way, I do enjoy atonal music. Also, I am intrigued by
electronic music, aleatory choral music, and other avante garde
explorations into sound not confined to the limits of human
perception of harmonics in small-number ratios. That is *not* what
this book is all about. What I am suggesting is that when we
experience tonal music, it would be wonderful to hear it as

accurately as possible in the simple tonal environment that nature provided.

Ironically, the invention that was supposed to have enhanced the excitement of free modulation actually blurred it. Most singers today, who routinely "learn their notes" from a keyboard, seldom thrill to a well-tuned chromatic leading tone as it propels the music into a distant tonal galaxy. They sing each note like every other note, like a keyboard, in innocent ignorance, unaware that they have been blindfolded to a potential kaleidoscope of harmonic brilliance.

Clearly, the reason this happens is because music theory and ear-training classes today focus more on notation and scales than on the physical nature of sound. This is very unfortunate, particularly when the major/minor system of music makes so much sense when analyzed in terms of its logic, symmetry and basis in simple physics. Memorization of scales and singing them on *do, re, mi,* did not provide me with a perceptual understanding of how music works, and I don't think it does for today's students either.

As an undergraduate music major, I got my *A* grades in music theory and history, graduated Magna Cum Laude, and went on to earn a Master's degree in music theory and a doctorate in music education. At no time during these years, did I read anything or hear a lecturer say anything that indicated that the major scale, or more precisely, the major/minor system, was an incredible breakthrough in that it fit the physical acoustic facts of the nature of sound better than any previous musical system. Sure, we were told about Rameau's great 17th century treatise on harmony; however, it was presented as a description of "common practice," that is, an observation and systematizing of what composers of that period had written. Since then, many brilliant theorists have expanded upon Rameau's work, written articles and textbooks based on his concepts of "functional harmony," and scores of musicians, composers and students have benefited from all of this scholarship. But *nothing* about practical acoustics and human perception of natural harmonic truth. Everyone bought tempered tuning as universal gospel.

Please understand, I have no problem with tempered tuning itself (at least for keyboards), or with all of the marvelous work that has been done in regard to describing musical common practice. My concern has to do with what *hasn't* been done re-garding the preservation and development of human aural per-ception and the physical nature of musical sound.

What I see today is music educators perpetuating the "eggs in row" concept of ear training, having beginning students practicing their *do-re-mi*'s in scalewise melodies. Discerning the difference between whole and half steps is a very difficult thing for beginners to do and is usually one of the *last* skills my students master. Combine that with the fact that early practice is almost always done with the aid of a tempered keyboard and you have the perfect pedagogical formula for frustration and failure.

Let's imagine a world in which youngsters have the tools and toys that provide them with early experiences of pure and simple sound relationships. These same youngsters then have the self confidence that follows success, and enjoy getting involved in making music that *sounds great*. Every basket is filled to the brim with tunes. Every rendition of "Happy Birthday" in every rest-aurant from here to heaven glows with sparkling harmonies. Those who choose to formalize their musical education are taught logical, practical ideas and systems that reflect the physical nature of sound, as well as the notational and stylistic traditions of the past. Keyboards are used with the full understanding that their tuning is compromised. Better yet, a computerized keyboard is invented that quickly analyzes the pitches it is playing and adjusts its own tuning to prevailing roots and tonics. Dreaming? I don't know. What do you think?

RHYTHM, METER AND OTHER IDEAS YOU CAN COUNT ON

I think I was a fairly decent music student when it came to performance of musical rhythms. Being a devoted Count Basie fan, I thought I had a pretty good idea of what a beat was. And being an admirer of Bartok and Brubeck, I could handle some fairly fancy metric patterns. Like most students who grew up around music, I seemed to have an intuitive ability to "understand" rhythm.

But, when I tried to express some of those early ideas in a formal way in my doctoral dissertation, *Conceptual Aspects of Rhythm*, I began to notice how fuzzy my concepts were. As a result, I began to give a great deal of thought to analyzing systematically how rhythm works. As was the case regarding matters of pitch discussed earlier, the "lies" I found regarding rhythm were largely a result of propagating "rules" and notational systems rather than dealing with basic perceptual and conceptual reality. Also, as with pitch, I found that "truths" were frequently available in the historical literature, but were largely ignored by teachers and textbooks. Here are the "lies" about rhythm and meter I believe to be most troublesome, along with the "truths" I found to be most enlightening.

Lie #13: A quarter note gets one beat.

Truth: Any note value can be assigned the beat.

American music students invariably begin their music reading lessons with meters in which the quarter note is the beat unit, and learn to perform a good deal of music in these meters. The problem is that many people discontinue their music studies believing that a quarter note *always* gets one beat.

Now, I know that much music can be successfully made with this incomplete information, and some folks get along for years depending on the postulate that "a quarter note gets one beat." Their teachers, who knew (hopefully) that other notes could be assigned to the beat unit and had planned to explain that fact in subsequent lessons, never got to share that information with their early dropouts. The "lie" in this case is the teacher's failure to *start* with a more universal truth.

Too often, students are asked to memorize empty words and rules when they have no idea what the words mean. On exam—inations, the students simply give the empty words back to the teacher and it is assumed that they have "learned the material." A better plan, when teaching meter, is to first show students *what it is*, and discuss quarter notes later. They need to be comfortable with the concepts of "two-ness" and "three-ness" and how these can be combined in metric structures. Good teaching should begin by helping students experience the thing to be learned, and *then* telling them what to call it. By teaching notational vocabulary and rules before basic perceptual concepts are secure, we end up with a generation of confused and, as you will see later, dangerous musicians.

A great many such students have appeared in my college classes. The routine goes something like this: I start with a dis—cussion of basic concepts of meter, and then talk about standard rhythmic notation in which each note value divides evenly into two of the next smaller value.

1 whole note	o
equals 2 half notes	♩ ♩
equals 4 quarter notes	♩ ♩ ♩ ♩
equals 8 eighth notes	♪♪ ♪♪ ♪♪ ♪♪
equals 16 sixteenth notes	♪♪♪♪ ♪♪♪♪ ♪♪♪♪ ♪♪♪♪

The point here is that the system is a *relational* one and no given note represents a fixed duration of time in terms of the clock. It is no coincidence that the language of fractions is used since note values fill up a given space much like fractions do. The "given space" in both systems is, of course, determined by other causes.

We next point out that *any* of these note values can be designated to represent one beat. Now that's a fairly simple concept, wouldn't you say? However, lurking beneath the level of conscious reason in many of my students' minds is the firm belief in the primacy of the quarter note, learned from earlier music studies, jamming the possibility of clear thought. The new words are heard, but the brewing conflict with the old concept has not yet surfaced.

Later, when performing a practice item in 2/2 meter (two half-note beats per measure), a student will see a measure having four quarter notes and, when asked, "How many beats in that measure?" will say, "Four." When I suggest that there are two beats in that measure, the student will respond, "But, I thought a quarter note gets one beat." At this point I usually get this weird smile on my face and move my head slowly from side to side.

Music publishers who sell to the mass market of music consumers know that music having a quarter note beat sells many more copies than music having other beat-unit designations. Church choir directors know that their singers (and frequently they themselves) feel more comfortable with a quarter note beat. Many public school music teachers are not all that emancipated from the domination of quarter notes either, and the amateur pop-music devotee who knows about non-quarter-note beat units is indeed a rare creature.

I suspect that some readers are now saying, "Come on, get out of your ivory tower. At least we have a lot of people making music with *some* kind of beat unit. Who cares if we use a quarter note more than others?!"

To a great extent, I suppose I agree. But what bothers me is the limited success afforded by this erroneous concept tends to short circuit the need for learning about the basic perceptual and systematic nature of musical meter, and creates confusion when *other* meters are encountered.

It is not only the student musician or the amateur singer/player who suffers from "quarter-note-itis." Some professional musicians as well seem to have been infected. A particularly troublesome example happened on the stage of the Hollywood Bowl one afternoon a few summers ago. The L.A. Jazz Choir, was rehearsing for a show that was to open that evening with Rosemary Clooney, Michael Feinstein and the L.A. Philharmonic. In order to conserve space, time and money, it was agreed that we would use the same instrumental back-up trio that was booked for the other acts.

It being an all-Gershwin show, I had arranged the tune *Liza* and jazzed it up with some interesting (and musical, I think) changing meters. I had made sure that all the meter changes were clearly marked. For example, when ¢ (same as 2/2) became 3/2 (to create a triple measure and turn the accent around), a $\downarrow = \downarrow$ was provided. When the ¢ changed to a Latin 4/4, a $\downarrow = \downarrow$ was shown. (If this is Greek, don't worry about it now.) The arrangement had previously been performed by a number of other instrumentalists on various LAJC performances. There was no reason to expect a problem.

When it was our turn to rehearse, we got the singers in place and passed out the charts to the trio. Since we only had about twenty minutes to rehearse three tunes, I needed to talk through the "Liza" chart with the musicians to make sure everything was clear.

It was quickly evident that the chart was *not* clear to the drummer. After a few whadda-y'-mean-here's, he began lecturing me on the correct way to notate music. My polite attempt to explain what I really *did* mean didn't seem to matter. His demeanor became more and more belligerent, until he stormed off the stage refusing to play the chart.

By this time, most of our rehearsal period is spent, the singers are still standing there waiting to rehearse, while the producer, Allan Sviridoff, is wondering what in the hell is going on, and I'm standing there in shock. Sviridoff, in his business suit and gleaming white sneakers, took command of the situation. With the calmest demeanor I have ever seen in such a tense situation, he made arrangements for us to use another drummer. The show went on with great success.

The drummer who refused to play the *Liza* chart is a respected studio musician with decades of experience. He is an "old pro." I'm sure he knew that to walk off the stage like that was a very unprofessional thing to do, even if I *was* all of the colorful things he called me as he left.

As I thought about it later, the only explanation that made any sense is that he realized he couldn't play the chart as it was written. He *had* to walk off stage. His lecture, I remembered, seemed to center around the idea that the quarter note should always be the beat unit, and in my chart it wasn't.

It doesn't really surprise me much that he could operate successfully for all those years in the studios. Most of the commercial things studio musicians are asked to play are written with (what else ?) a quarter note beat.

Music theory textbooks haven't helped much to alleviate the problem. Rarely is there an early discussion of what the concept of meter is and how note values relate to it. Invariably, the first illustrations of meter are provided with *only* quarter notes as the primary beat.

Sometimes, in a quiet moment, I wonder if my first music teacher really *did* know that a quarter note doesn't always get one beat. Or maybe he felt I just wasn't mature enough to handle the information. I guess I'll never know for sure.

Lie #14: The top number tells how many beats are in each measure.

Truth: The top number tells how many of a specified note value are in each measure. The number of beats is determined by other considerations.

What we are talking about here is the *meter signature*. That's the two numbers, one above the other, that you see at the beginning of a piece of music. It tells the reader what the underlying metric structure is in that piece. It's sometimes called the *time signature*, but I think that name is vague and misleading. "Time" connotes the whole temporal aspect of music, including tempo and other specific aspects. It also erroneously suggests that "clock time" is somehow involved. "Meter" is right to the point.

Like the previous lie, this one is sometimes true, but is very often recited, memorized, and passed on from generation to generation without the knowledge that under some circumstances the top number is *not* the number of beats per measure. The con—

fusion, I believe, comes from a fuzzy concept or ambiguous application of the terms "beat" and "accent," as well as from not realizing that meter consists of *more* than one pulse series.

For example, the tune *Seventy Six Trombones* has two beats per measure yet the top number of its meter signature is 6. In this case, the top number doesn't refer to the beat, but rather to the parts, or divisions, of the beat.

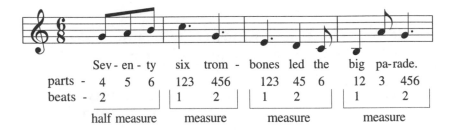

"So," you may be thinking, "if there are two beats per measure in *Seventy Six Trombones* why not use 2 as the top number? The answer is that the note selected as the beat unit must divide into three equal parts. "So divide it into three parts, then," you say. "What's the big problem?"

The problem is that, in our notational system, a given note won't divide into three equal notes of a smaller size. For example, if you divided a circle into three equal parts, you would call each part a "third." That may work for circles but it doesn't work for notes. We don't have "third-notes" in our system. Similarly, if you divide a quarter of a circle into three equal parts, you call each part a "twelfth." But we don't have "twelfth-notes" in our system.

"Well why not?" you ask. "If we want and need third notes and twelfth notes, why not invent them? If this would simplify musical notation, let's go ahead and do it."

Well, first of all, we wouldn't be the first to try it. Musicians in the Gothic period (c. 1150-1450) developed a very sophisticated system of rhythmic notation that included both duple and triple divisions of the beat.

And, second of all, it doesn't work very well. Well, actually it worked fine for the Gothics as long as they didn't mix too many duple and triple elements in the same music. But, mixing eighth notes, quarter notes, and half notes with third notes and twelfth notes would lead to some very complicated notation. We came up with a better way. More about that later.

Although we didn't adopt the Gothics' notational system, it will help to look at their basic concept of meter. The Gothics, being very religious and very Christian, called triple elements *perfectum* (as in the Holy Trinity) and duple elements *imperfectum* (as in a two-legged human doing a two-beat dance). While some of us may not appreciate the basis on which they selected their terms, we can all appreciate their very logical and accurate description of the basic perceptual nature of musical meter.

Their system was based on the idea (and practical observation) that a given pulse series can be *grouped* in regular sets of twos or threes and can also be *divided* into sets of twos or threes. These two relationships (groupings and divisions) can be combined in four ways, creating four basic multi-level metric structures. Like "minor mode," the basic concept of musical meter is pretty simple, but it gets confusing when we attempt to write it down in traditional music notation. So, let's start with a definition of the basic ingredient of meter: *beat* (and it's synonym, *pulse*).

Beat: a series of regularly recurrent events that are conceived and/or perceived as real or imaginary kines–thetic events.

That may sound a bit academic, but every word was carefully chosen. Let me tell you why each word is vital to a clear definition and an understanding of beat and meter.

The word "series" is important because a single event doesn't create any flow. It takes at least two events to know what the time interval is in the series. Once established however, the time inter–val is predictable by the perceiver and the series can be maintained with a modest amount of thought or effort. With a little practice, it can be placed on "automatic," leaving the conscious attention free to attend to more interesting matters in the music.

The words "regularly recurrent" are vital. If the events are not perceived as equally spaced, the series is not a true pulse. For example, the reading of prose is not likely to suggest a pulse series in that the time intervals between the events (syllables, accents, etc.) are not symmetrical and predictable. The reading may contain some rhythmic elements (a sense of flow, for example) but usually not a pulse.

One might think that *tempo rubato*, the practice of slightly slowing or hurrying the beat, as one would do in a very expres–sive passage of Romantic style music, would argue against this definition. Actually, it proves the point. Rubato is simply com–bining *two* concepts: "regularity of recurrent beats" and "regularity in the rate of slowing or hurrying." If the rubato is jerky or sudden, the flow is destroyed. Again, no regularity, no beat.

The word "events" was selected instead of "sounds", "clicks," "taps" or other "musical" terms because pulse can also be per–ceived in media other than sound (light flashes, bouncing balls, back scratching, arm swinging, etc.), or simply imagined without physical existence.

The word "kinesthetic" is included for a very important rea-son. In the 1920's and '30s, music psychologists were very much interested in discovering what causes humans to develop a sense of pulse. They conducted experiments with heart beats, brain waves, and anything else that appeared to suggest regularity of occurrence. What they discovered is that humans seem to learn a sense of pulse through physical movement--like walking. At a fairly early age, we learn that if we don't get our foot out in front at exactly the right time, we stumble and skin our noses. Although we didn't know it at the time, we were actually having our first music lessons while we were learning to walk. The fancy term for muscle movement is *kinesthetic*, thus its inclusion in our def-inition.

The terms "conceived" and "perceived" apply, of course, to the composer (and his representative, the performer) and the listener respectively. Remember, we are talking communication here, are we not?

You may want to go back and reread the whole definition now and see if it all makes sense. If it still seems a bit fuzzy, read on and let's see if we can clarify further. Let's get back to the Goth-ics' concept of meter. The Gothics were very much aware of one aspect of the nature of meter that current theory textbooks frequently ignore -- the fact that a meter is actually a composite of related pulses.

A single pulse series by itself is a simple (and eventually boring) thing:

pulse - | | | | | | | | |

The Gothics discovered that by combining and coordinating a given pulse with another pulse that is exactly two or three times slower, a more interesting flow is achieved.

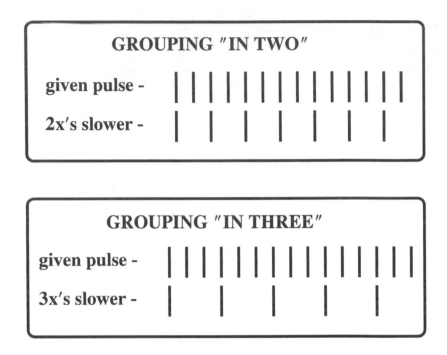

To get the feel of this flow, try tapping a "given pulse" with your hand (about walking speed) and tapping your foot on every third hand tap. Notice that the foot is also keeping a pulse, having its own regularity of time interval. Stop your hand tap while continuing the foot tap, but keep *imagining* the hand tap. Now stop the foot tap and continue both pulses in your imagination.

Now, try the same thing with a two to one ratio; that is, tap your foot on every *second* hand tap. Again, stop tapping and continue the combined pulses in your imagination.

Did you notice that, as the pattern began to flow, its *quan-titative* aspect began to be replaced by a *qualitative* one. That is, you no longer had to *count* the beats. In your two-to-one perform-ance, for example, you simply maintained a feeling flow like a windshield wiper -- back-forth-back-forth-back-forth. Life is filled with examples of the qualitative concept of "two-ness": spacial (up-down, in-out, left-right), logical (right-wrong, good-bad, yes-no), temporal (past-future), etc.

Examples of the qualitative concept of "three-ness" are not so plentiful. After "triangle," "Hegelian dialectic," and attempts to include the elusive "present," they peter out pretty fast. Never-theless, it is quite clear that people *can* develop a kinesthetic feel for three-ness. It's a little harder to create and maintain than two-ness, but then no one said life was easy. When my students have a hard time identifying triple metric patterns, I tell them that if it doesn't feel like a windshield wiper it must be "that other one."

As was mentioned earlier, the Gothics regarded the number three as having religious significance, so meters having a triple ratio were called *tempus perfectum*. They indicated this metric flow with a "perfect" circle. Meters having a duple ratio were called *tempus imperfectum* and were indicated by a half circle. Our modern terms for these patterns are *triple meter* and *duple meter*.

tempus perfectum
(triple meter)

tempus imperfectum
(duple meter)

A little later we will look at the Gothics' concept of *divisions* of beats, which will help to clarify our little meter-signature problem with *Seventy Six Trombones*. But first, it will be helpful to deal with another "lie" that interferes with the development of a clear concept of musical meter.

Lie #15: Notes that fall on strong metric beats are to be performed with a stress because they are more important than the notes on weaker beats.

Truth: Metric accent is silent and therefore does not necessarily affect audible performance details.

A few years ago, I was in San Francisco to give expert testimony in a court case involving John Fogerty and Fantasy Records. Fantasy was contending that Fogerty had based his new song *Old Man Down The Road* on his previous song *Run Through The Jungle*. *Run* was written for and recorded by Creedence Clearwater Revival and owned by Fantasy Records.

Fantasy's lawyer was quite knowledgeable about music and his questions during his cross examination of my testimony gave evidence of that fact. One of his goals was to get me to agree that in 4/4 meter the music on the first beat of each measure was accented, and therefore "more important" than the other beats, and that music on the third beat was next most important because it had a secondary accent. My response was, "Not necessarily." He was not pleased.

His point was to suggest that the pickup notes in *Old Man* were not as important as the notes on the "strong" beats, which (he felt) would make the two songs more alike.

Later in the proceedings, Fogerty performed *Mack The Knife* without pickup notes. If you know the song, you know that its most significant melodic notes *are* the pickup notes. That pretty much settled the matter of the musical importance of pickup notes. The matter of how "accents" relate to meter was *not* settled in court, however. After John's performance, it didn't seem particularly critical to the case.

But the lawyer's notion about accents on first and third beats is a very popular one, however, and its clarification is most critical to understanding meter. This "lie" is included in almost every basic theory textbook, and I feel it causes considerable confusion. The problem, I think, has to do with fuzzy concepts of what a musical accent *is*. So, let's try to minimize musical preconceptions and begin this discussion with a simple *non*-musical definition.

Accent: a feature that stands out from its surroundings.

I think the confusion comes from not realizing that there are *different* kinds of accents in music. Accents created by *loudness* are the type most people think of when the word is used. It's the only type of accent that has a notational sign (>), so it's easy to get the idea that it is the only one there is. When this sign is en–countered in music, the performer is being instructed to make that note louder than the surrounding notes so it will stand out. The amount of contrast is up to the musical taste of the performer as he senses the character of the phrase.

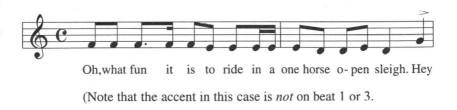

Oh, what fun   it   is to ride in a one horse o- pen sleigh. Hey

(Note that the accent in this case is *not* on beat 1 or 3.)

That type of accent is called a *dynamic* accent.

Here's another type. Notice how accents are created in this series of notes.

The longer notes are heard as accents by virtue of their contrast to the shorter notes. This type of accent is called *agogic* . Notice that it still works even when you start with the short notes.

Another type of accent can be created by pitch patterns. Notice that, in the following example, accent patterns are created even though the note durations are even and regular. We can call these *melodic* accents.

Because the pitches that are different from the repeated pitch happen on every third note, a feeling of triple meter is felt, or as the Gothics would say, tempus perfectum.

In this case, the melodic accents are partly *responsible* for suggesting a metric pattern because they are regular and can be predicted. But the metric accent itself is something *other than* the musical events that can be heard in the music.

Do you remember when we were tapping hands and feet to create duple and triple ratios between a given pulse and a related pulse two or three times slower? Remember also that we were able to maintain these meters in our imagination without actually performing them? That silent sense of flow of related pulses we called meter, therefore the "accents" that we experience while maintaining a meter are called *metric* accents. In other words, we don't *hear* metric accents, we *think* them. Or more precisely, we *feel* them.

Metric accents occur when pulses at different levels occur simultaneously. In order to show how this works, let's add a few more related pulse series to our meter. In addition to our given pulse and our grouping pulse, let's add one twice as fast (dividing each given pulse into two equal pulses). Now let's add another one twice as slow as our grouping pulse. We now have a graphic presentation of the "lawyer's measure," the concept that was under consideration in the Fogerty matter.

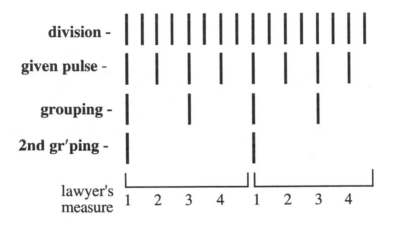

Notice that beat one of the lawyer's measure occurs simultaneously in *all four* of the pulse levels, which in effect makes that event "feel" stronger -- or accented -- in contrast to the other beats. Notice also that beat three is similarly reinforced, but only by *three* pulse levels, creating the lawyer's "secondary accent."

Now here is the important thing about metric accents. They are *not* louder than other beats. They can't be, since they exist only in the imagination. They are *silent accents which exist only by virtue of the combination of pulse levels flowing in the imagination.* They may (and frequently do) occur in sync with the audible ac‐cents in the music, but they are not the same thing.

To be sure, a composer usually supplies the listener with an audible and appropriate "oom-pah-pah" or "oom-pah" to get him started, but the responsibility for maintaining the kinesthetic metric continuity is then largely left to the listener, especially in sophisticated art music. Once a metric pattern is established, the composer can either use audible accent patterns which basically agree with the established meter, or he can create contrasting patterns that conflict with the continuing sense of metric flow.

A composer uses many accent types, perhaps more intuitively than analytically, to create musical phrases in many styles and moods. When the various accent types occur simultaneously, the effect is usually smooth and peaceful. Here the melodic, agogic, dynamic and metric accents are all in sync.

When one type of accent occurs in conflict with another, some interesting rhythmic patterns are created. We call these rhythms *syncopations*. In the following phrase, melodic and agogic accents are in conflict with the metric accents.

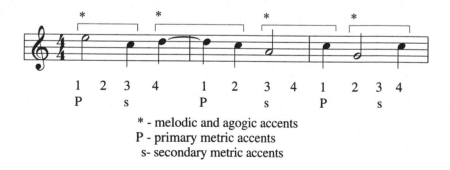

* - melodic and agogic accents
P - primary metric accents
s - secondary metric accents

It is assumed in the preceding illustration that the "feeling" of 4/4 has previously been established for the listener. The audible accents here, which would fit nicely into a 3/4 meter, create con–flict with the prevailing 4/4 meter.

In the following illustration, the melodic and dynamic accents vie for supremacy over the metric and agogic accents.

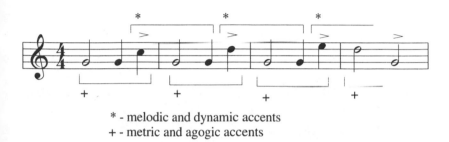

* - melodic and dynamic accents
+ - metric and agogic accents

In this popular Scott Joplin ragtime tune, syncopation is created by the interplay of melodic, agogic and metric accents.

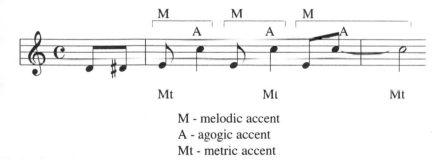

M - melodic accent
A - agogic accent
Mt - metric accent

Like so many experiences in life, musical rhythm is a bit more complex than one might realize. When we were very young, we organized our experiences in broad, general concepts -- "car," "go bye-bye," "daddy." As we matured we became auto mechanics, toured Europe and our parents became ordinary humans with both good and not-so-good characteristics. Perhaps that is why a Beet–

hoven symphony is heard by a youngster as "nice music" and by a veteran listener as "profound." In any case, I sincerely hope you won't toss the word "accent" around carelessly. Remember, metric accent is a *silent* event created by the simultaneous occurrences of pulses within a system of related series.

Lie #16: There is a wide variety of meters.

Truth: There are four basic metric structures.

Some of my theory students seem to have the idea that you can combine any two numbers and come up with a meter signature. These folks appear to be swimming in a sea of endless possibilities. The truth is that there are only *four* ways to combine the factors 2 and 3 in three levels of related pulses. Let's take another look at the Gothics' concept of meter. We noted earlier (on page 128) that when they combined a given pulse with a slower one in a ratio of two or three they called it *tempus imperfectum* and *tempus perfectum*, respectively. This, in effect, *grouped* the given pulses into duple or triple meters.

When they *divided* the beat into two or three parts, they called it *prolatium* (pro-laht-si-um) *imperfectum* and *prolatium perfectum*.

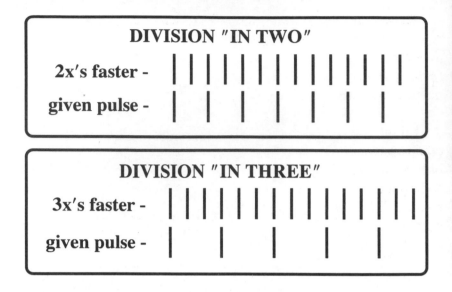

So, the Gothics viewed meter as having two metric relation-ships (actually three, but let's keep it simple): (1) the ratio between a given pulse and its grouping (*tempus*), and (2) the ratio between a given pulse and its division (*prolatium*). Here's how they com-bined these factors into their basic meter types.

Remember that in the Gothics' system the full circle meant *tempus perfectum* (three beats in a group, or triple meter) and the half circle meant *tempus imperfectum* (two beats in a group, or duple meter). Their method of indicating *prolatium perfectum* was to place a dot in the circle (or half circle) and show no dot in the circle (or half circle) to indicate *prolatium imperfectum*.

⊙   ◯

prolatium perfectum (triple div.)   prolatium imperfectum (duple div.)
tempus perfectum (triple grp.)   tempus perfectum (triple grp.)

⊂•   ⊂

prolatium perfectum (triple div.)   prolatium imperfectum (duple div.)
tempus imperfectum (duple grp.)   tempus imperfectum (duple grp.)

These four metric combinations are what we call a logically "closed system." That is, there are no more than these four ways to combine groupings (*tempus*) of twos and threes with divisions (*prolatium*) of twos and threes. So, you see, the basic nature of musical meter is actually a pretty simple thing.

I think the confusion started when we went to an exclusively duple system of notation. Perhaps this would be a good time to get back to *Seventy Six Trombones* and its relationship to the trouble-some statement, "the top number tells how many beats are in each measure." Remember that the problem centers around the fact that because our notational system is a duple one, there is no apparent way to divide a single note into three parts.

One way the problem has been solved is to use triplets. This is a handy device that musicians developed to impose three note values in place of two of the same denomination. For example, a quarter note normally divides into *two* eighth notes; but by placing a numeral 3 over a beat, one is permitted to divide that quarter note beat into *three* eighth-notes. Mathematical heresy you say? I suppose so, but it works pretty well.

Sev-en-ty   six   trom bones led— the big— pa- rade.—

However, if one has an extended composition with many triple divisions of the beat, it would be awkward and cumbersome to place a 3 over most of the beats. The Gothics would have solved the problem with ease -- simply indicate that *Seventy Six Trombones* had a *tempus imperfectum* and a *prolatium perfectum*, by putting a dotted half-circle at the beginning of the music. Some-times I wonder if we really progress through the centuries, or just simply change. (Didn't John Cage say something like that?)

Our modern solution was pretty clever, however. It's as sim–
ple as the paper clip, and equally as useful. Follow this closely: IF
A SINGLE NOTE DIVIDES INTO TWO PARTS, A NOTE AND
A HALF WILL DIVIDE INTO THREE PARTS. Ta-daa!! That's
it. Composers simply placed a dot after any note they wanted to
increase by half its value and the triple division was made pos–
sible.

So, by using a dotted note to represent the beat, we can write
"Seventy Six Trombones" without writing triplets throughout the
manuscript.

Now, let's write a meter signature in front of the music so
anyone who reads it will know which of the four basic metric
structures we are using. Since the dotted half-circle is a bit out of
date, that probably won't do. So, let's try the standard rule "the
top number tells how many beats in a measure." Since the group–
ing (*tempus*) in *Trombones* is in two, we will use 2 as the top
number of our signature.

Now we need to supply the bottom number of the signature.
The traditional rule is that "the bottom number tells what kind of
note represents one beat." So we'll write in the number that
represents a dotted quarter note. Wait a minute! What *is* the
number that represents a dotted quarter note? Is there one?

Perhaps we had better first look at bottom numbers that *don't*
need to divide the beat in thirds. In meters that have beats that

divide in two parts (*prolatium imperfectum*), this is done with ease by using an 8 to indicate eighth notes, 4 to indicate quarter notes, 2 to indicate half notes, etc. Thus, "Yankee Doodle" can be written in any of these meters.

(No! The top one is *not* faster than the others.)

That seems simple enough. In fact, this type of meter (*prolatium imperfectum*) is traditionally called *simple meter.* Just count the number of beats in a group (two or three) and the beats will divide into two of the next smallest denomination whenever required by the composer's idea. No problem.

In the case of *Trombones* however, we need a number that will divide into three equal parts. So what number shall we use as the bottom number of the meter signature? Since the note value we used above was a dotted quarter, how about 4 1/2?

Sev - en - ty   six   trom - bones

No, I guess not. It looks a bit strange. Hmm...let's see... Since the dot equals half the value of the note it follows, how about 4/8?

Sev - en - ty   six   trom - bones

No, huh? Well, suppose we break with tradition and, instead of using a number to represent the beat unit, use the *dotted note itself.*

Sev - en - ty   six   trom - bones

Pretty clever, eh? It's simple and easy to understand. It does exactly what a meter signature is supposed to do -- it says there are two dotted quarter notes (or the equivalent) per measure. And best of all, it gives us a logical way to indicate *prolatium perfectum* (triple division).

Before you get too excited, I probably should tell you that a German composer, Carl Orff (1895-1982), already introduced the idea. However, it didn't catch on. Too bad! He was consistent in using his idea, employing it in simple meter as well. In Orff terms, the four basic Gothic meters would be written like this:

$$\odot = \dfrac{3}{\text{𝅗𝅥.}} \quad \text{or} \quad \dfrac{3}{\text{♩.}} \quad \text{or} \quad \dfrac{3}{\text{♪.}} \quad \text{etc.}$$

$$\bigcirc = \dfrac{3}{\text{𝅗𝅥}} \quad \text{or} \quad \dfrac{3}{\text{♩}} \quad \text{or} \quad \dfrac{3}{\text{♪}} \quad \text{etc.}$$

$$\big({\cdot} = \dfrac{2}{\text{𝅗𝅥.}} \quad \text{or} \quad \dfrac{2}{\text{♩.}} \quad \text{or} \quad \dfrac{2}{\text{♪.}} \quad \text{etc.}$$

$$\big(= \dfrac{2}{\text{𝅗𝅥}} \quad \text{or} \quad \dfrac{2}{\text{♩}} \quad \text{or} \quad \dfrac{2}{\text{♪}} \quad \text{etc.}$$

It seems a shame that Orff's signatures didn't become the standard way of indicating meters. It is so simple and logical. I guess tradition is still a stronger force in the world than logic and simplicity.

(It was, in fact, Orff's lack of success with this great idea that made me realize that I probably wouldn't get very far with my "better" idea for minor key signatures. I wonder if he learned to live with failure as gracefully as I have.)

So how do we write a meter signature that will indicate two beats per measure, each beat dividing into three parts? Simple. We count the *parts* instead of the beats. Well, actually not "simple" in the sense we used it above -- as in "simple meter." It's traditionally called *compound* meter.

This is how it works. If you combine a number of simple/–triple measures and add up the *parts* , instead of the beats, you get a meter signature that can be expressed in two whole numbers, the top one telling "how many" and the bottom one telling "how many *whats*."

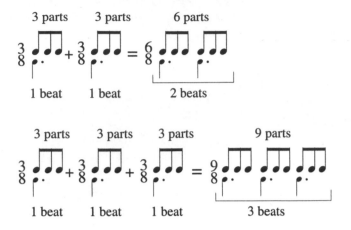

Pretty neat, huh? If the beat selected is a dotted half note, the "parts" to be counted would be the quarter notes.

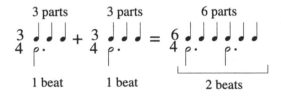

"Why," you ask, "do we need to go through all of this darn compounding if the music can be written in simple triple?" The answer is, "we *don't* have to." For example, the waltz is traditionally written in 3/4 meter even though it has a duple grouping of main beats.

Notice that the body feel, or kinesthetic flow, of a waltz places a metric accent on alternate measures, creating a *tempus imperf–*

ectum (duple meter). It would make perfect sense to write the waltz in compound duple meter. We'll combine two 3/4's into sets of 6/4's.

Or it could be written in the more popular 6/8.

The advantage of writing music having a triple division (*pro–latium perfectum*) in compound meter is that it shows the number of beats in a measure -- two beats (*tempus imperfectum*) or three beats (*tempus perfectum*). 3/8 meter (simple triple) doesn't show how many beats (measures) are in a grouping.

6/8 meter does.

Notice that the metric structure is the same in either case.

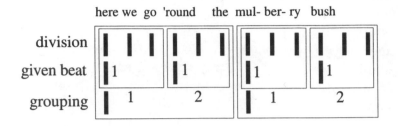

Again, 3/8 doesn't show the metric grouping of beats in this song.

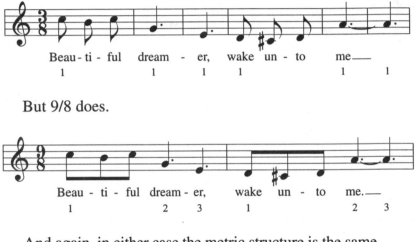

But 9/8 does.

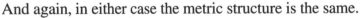

And again, in either case the metric structure is the same.

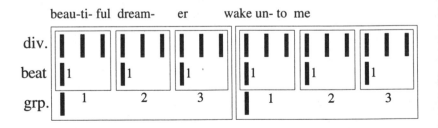

Whether to compound or not to compound -- that is the question. Actually it is a matter of tradition. Beethoven wrestled with

this problem when he wrote the scherzo of his ninth symphony. To understand his position, a little background will be helpful.

During the late eighteenth century, when young Ludwig was writing his first symphony, it was the custom to write a minuet as the third movement. The minuet, a predecessor of the waltz, was a triple meter dance. Although Beethoven's tempo was a bit fast for a minuet, it still had an *tempus perfectum* in that the main beats were grouped in threes.

By the time Beethoven wrote his ninth symphony, some profound changes had taken place--both in the world and in Beet--hoven. France was becoming a republic, powdered wigs were out, and gut-wrenching emotion was in. The classical minuet was by then old fashioned and would serve no artistic purpose in the thoroughly romantic ninth symphony.

But, even a revolutionary like Beethoven could not completely ignore tradition. He had, in earlier symphonies, transformed the third-movement *tempus-perfectum* minuet into a *prolatium-per-fectum* scherzo by speeding up the tempo. Even though the faster tempo caused the triple meter to be felt "in one" (even faster than the waltz), he couldn't bring himself to use a compound meter. Tradition wouldn't hear of it.

In the *Ninth*, the tempo of the scherzo was blazingly fast. The 3/4 measures flew past the players eyes so fast there was danger of getting lost in the blur of quarter notes. But Beethoven's allegiance to tradition would not be broken. Instead of giving in to compounding, he grouped the measures into a *tempus imper-fectum* by numbering them.

It worked! Now the players could see and feel the metric flow that Fantasy's lawyer would describe in court many years later, in this case with a prolatium perfectum (triple division).

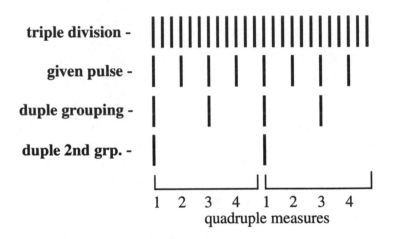

The diagram shows that, had Beethoven been less a tradi‑tionalist, he might have written his scherzo in a compound meter. If he wanted to be faithful to his quadruple grouping, he might have selected 12/4 meter.

Or 12/8, which is visually clearer, because eighth notes can be beamed together by beats.

As the diagram also shows, he could have chosen 6/4 or 6/8, since these are based on the same metric structure as 12/4 and 12/8. For some reason that is unclear to me, tradition has favored using 6/8 for faster tempos and 12/8 for slower tempos. Logic would argue for just the opposite, since faster tempos would allow for a stronger kinesthetic feel of the quad-measure barline and slower tempos would spread them too far apart.

Perhaps the tradition relates back to the baroque dance called a gigue, or the more recent 6/8 march, both of which are fast in tempo and are traditionally written in compound duple meter.

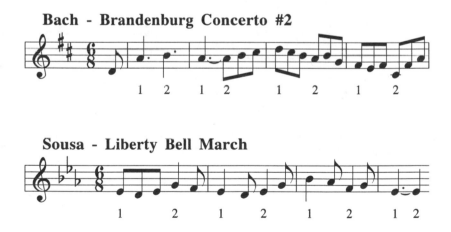

Come to think of it, even a march in simple duple is traditionally written in 2/4 when it is in parade tempo and 4/4 when it is in the slower processional style.

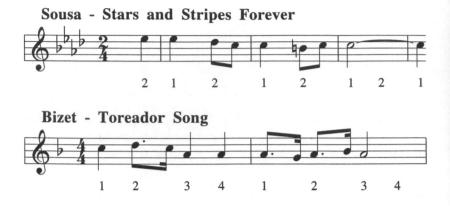

Sousa - Stars and Stripes Forever

Bizet - Toreador Song

Oh, well. I guess one shouldn't expect to understand every-thing. Especially tradition!

So, here's the bottom line. There are only *four* basic metric structures. The reason there appears to be such a variety of meters is that a composer can choose from a number of options in notating a musical idea. If no triple pulse ratio is present, the writer can use any note value for the given beat and simply count the number of those beats in each group. When a triple ratio is included in the metric structure, he has to make a decision. He can assign a note value to the triple pulse level and write it in simple triple, even if that note value is not the main beat. Or he can group the triple pulses into "sets" and use a compound meter. In both cases, there is also the option to double the number of pulses in each measure. It doesn't affect the audible character of the music in any way.

Oh? You think it does? Read on, my friend.

Lie #17: Quadruple meter has a differ-
ent "feel" from duple meter and
therefore each is sometimes
more appropriate for
certain music.

Truth: Combining measures for convenience
of notation has no effect on the
"feel" of the music.

I have heard sophisticated musicians discuss the subtle dif–
ferences between duple and quadruple meter (but usually after
quite a few beers). If you are suffering from this illogical concept,
perhaps this discussion will help.

Let's take two traditional melodies that, to me, have the same
musical "feel"--*Old MacDonald* and *Yankee Doodle*. Have you
noticed that most published versions of *Old MacDonald* are in 4/4
while most published versions of *Yankee Doodle* are 2/4?

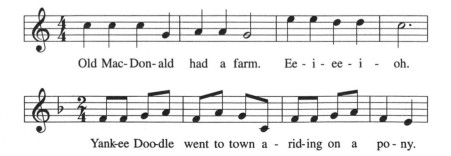

Why not the other way around?

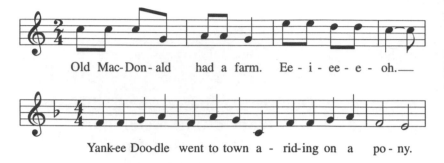

Remember, meter is a silent and imaginary combination of *felt* pulse series related in twos and/or threes. Four is simply a nota–tional compounding of two sets of two. Here's the "lawyer's measure" we looked at earlier.

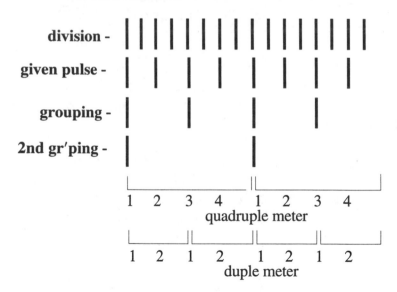

Every second measure of duple meter is still felt as a metric stress. Do you still think there is a musical difference between 2/4 and 4/4? If so, you are probably still confusing dynamic accents with metric accents. If you think *Old MacDonald* is better served by 4/4 because each quarter note is more evenly stressed than in the 4/4 version of *Yankee Doodle*, you just proved my point. Your argument has to do with *performance* values rather than metric values. In other words, the dynamics (loudness contrasts) of the phrase suggested to you that four was more appropriate than two. But don't despair -- the great Beethoven was hung up by traditional concepts, too.

So let's pull all of this discussion together into some organization that will be useful in terms of current musical practices. We can express the Gothics' four basic metric patterns in today's notation by using these four "top numbers": 2, 3, 6 and 9.

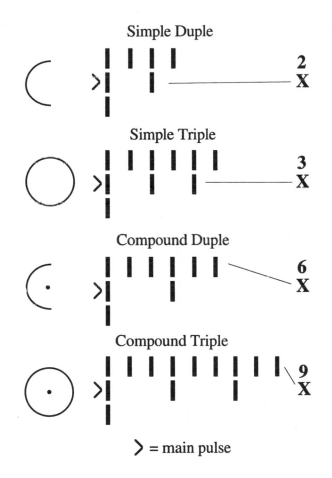

$\rangle$ = main pulse

All other modern meter signatures are simply combinations of these four basic systems. (No, this isn't algebra. The x stands for "any note value." Well, I guess it's sort of like algebra.)

$$\frac{4}{x} = \frac{2}{x} + \frac{2}{x}$$

$$\frac{5}{x} = \frac{2}{x} + \frac{3}{x} \text{ or } \frac{3}{x} + \frac{2}{x}$$

$$\frac{7}{x} = \frac{2}{x} + \frac{2}{x} + \frac{3}{x} \text{ or } \frac{3}{x} + \frac{2}{x} + \frac{2}{x} \text{ or } \frac{2}{x} + \frac{3}{x} + \frac{2}{x}$$

$$\frac{12}{x} = \frac{6}{x} + \frac{6}{x}$$

$$\frac{15}{x} = \frac{6}{x} + \frac{9}{x} \text{ or } \frac{9}{x} + \frac{6}{x}$$

Meters having mixed *prolatium*, or division of 5, 7, some 9s, 11, etc.), are also based on the four basic systems. However, when mixing twos and threes at the division level while main-taining regularity of that pulse, the normal "given" pulse is no longer a true pulse in that the events are not equally spaced in time.

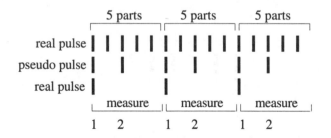

The signature in such meters are like compound meters in that the top number counts the parts, not the beats.

$$\frac{5}{4} \text{ or } \frac{5}{8} \text{ or } \frac{5}{16} \text{ etc.}$$

In such meters, the conductor will beat the pseudo pulse even though it is not an even spacing of events. He and the performers are controlling the flow of the music by concentrating on the division level pulse, keeping it even, and thinking in terms of alternating sets of little twos and threes.

It should be clear by now that a composer has considerable latitude in deciding what meter signature will best communicate his music to a performer. If the metric flow contains no triple ratios, in other words simple duple, a top number of 2 or 4 over any simple note value will serve very well.

Of course, if you want to *sell* your music, you probably should use a quarter note beat.

If your musical idea contains at least one triple pulse ratio, your choices must be made somewhat more carefully. If it is only the grouping that creates the triple ratio, simple triple will be a practical choice.

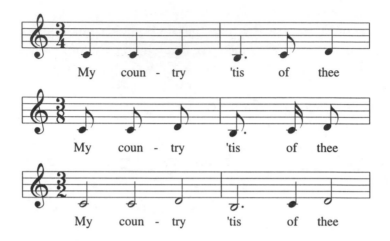

However, if you want the feeling of accent on every *second* measure to be evident in the written music, you might consider a compound duple, even in slow tempo where the "parts" are felt as the main beat.

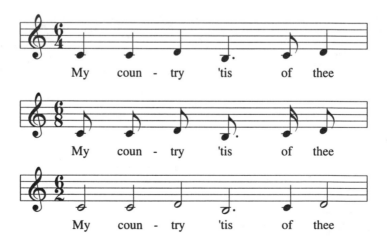

I know that choice is sort of weird, but some people do it. 12 is also a logical possibility but, thank God, hardly anybody does it.

If your music has two main beats to the group, each dividing into three parts, compound duple is the practical choice.

Simple triple is not out of the question, however. Remember the waltz?

But if your music has two adjoining triple levels, you really have little practical choice other than compound triple.

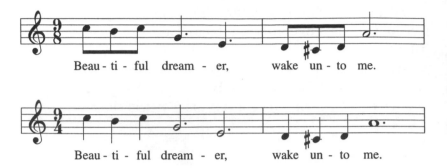

Beau - ti - ful dream - er,   wake un - to me.

Beau - ti - ful dream - er,   wake un - to me.

Sometimes a musical idea contains both a duple and a triple division of the beat. In such cases, use the meter that needs the least number of triplets or duplets.

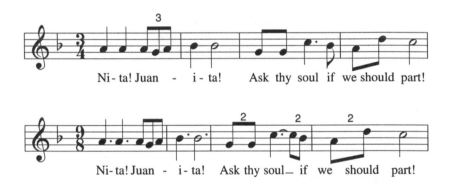

Ni - ta! Juan - i - ta!   Ask thy soul if we should part!

Ni - ta! Juan - i - ta!   Ask thy soul_ if we should part!

Clearly, the 3/4 meter is less complicated.

Here's an interesting problem. Suppose your name is Maurice Ravel and you have this great rhythmic idea for a Bolero that goes like this.

What meter would you use? Your choice should make the metric flow clear to the performer. So let's see how the rhythmic pattern is organized. If we assume the beat unit to be the dotted quarter note, the music seems to group in two's.

The grouping of the measures, however, seem to be in threes, due to the rhythms in measures one and two being repeated in measures four and five. So, do we pull a Beethoven trick and simply number the measures?

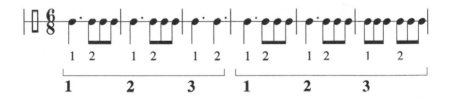

The real Maurice Ravel solved the problem this way. Since the strong sense of a slow triple grouping was appropriate to the melody, he opted for simple triple, writing out the triplets in the second division level.

The pattern graphs out like this. (I threw in a 6/8 pattern for comparison.)

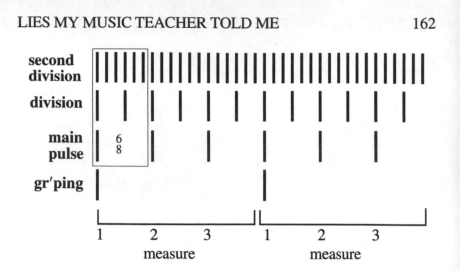

He could have written it in 6/8. Would that have changed the "feel"? Not even a little bit! At least no more so than Beethoven's scherzo from 3/4 to 12/8.

METER SUMMARY

So, where does all of this land? Hopefully, it has settled into a clear and simple concept of what musical meter is and how it relates to notation. But just to nail it all down, let's recap the main points in rather precise terms.

1. Meter is a combination of three (or more) related pulse series in ratios of two-to-one and/or three-to-one. It functions as an imaginary (as opposed to auditory) "kinesthetic" flow, providing a temporal matrix by which one can measure (relatively) the rhythmic events in a musical work.

2. Structures having three pulses in a group are called *triple meter*, and structures having two pulses in a group are called *duple meter*.

3. Structures in which a given beat divides into two parts are called *simple meter*, and those in which the given beat divides into three parts are called *compound meter*.

4. There are four basic metric structures:

    a) grouping a given pulse series in twos, each pulse dividing into two parts.

    b) grouping a given pulse series in threes, each pulse dividing into two parts.

    c) grouping a given pulse series in twos, each pulse dividing into three parts.

    d) grouping a given pulse series in threes, each pulse dividing into three parts.

5. Because our system of rhythmic notation is a duple one, only simple meters can be expressed by counting the number of given beats (top number) and assigning to the given beat *any* simple note value (bottom number). Therefore, a top number of 2 or 3 indicates simple meter.

6. Compound meters must have a dotted note assigned to the given beat (in order to divide it into three equal parts), and there–fore, because a dotted note value cannot be expressed as a simple number, it cannot be used in the signature as the bottom number. However, the collective *parts* of the beats, since they are simple notes, can be counted and used in the signature. Therefore, a top number of 6 or 9 indicates compound meter.

7. At the option of the composer, duple or triple measures can be combined symmetrically into larger measures, such as quad–ruple and sextuple measures, indicated by meter signatures having top numbers of 4, 6, 12, and (logically, but rarely) 18. This does not change the basic metric structure of the music, so it is purely a matter of notational preference.

8. Asymmetrically combined patterns (such as quintuple and septuple meters) will contain a pseudo pulse (non regular) at some level, and regularity of tempo is dependent on other (regular) pulse levels, usually the one next faster than the pseudo pulse.

9. Metric accents are caused by the simultaneous occurrences of pulses at different levels within a metric structure. These are *silent* kinesthetic patterns, not to be confused with auditory accents that occur in the actual musical sounds.

10. When auditory accents conflict with metric accents, the resultant rhythms are called *syncopations*.

Now, I hope that recap wasn't too academic and stuffy. I wanted to get everything in that was essential and yet use the words economically. The most important thing, however, is to realize that understanding meter, like understanding pitch relations, depends on focusing on *the thing itself* before focusing on the notation we use to represent it.

CODA

Dear reader, I hope this has been worth your time and effort. If you are one of those who has been "lied" *to*, my wish is that you found some ideas that will put you more in touch with practical music making. If you are a music educator who has been perpetuating the traditional "lies," perhaps you will re-think some of your teaching practices and turn the focus toward *real* music instead of empty notational rituals. If you are a practical musician who has been nodding your head in affirmation all through this book, I hope you will come out of the closet and make some noise.

This certainly has been a worthwhile exercise for me. It always helps to put ideas down on paper when you want to clarify them for yourself. And clarifying ideas is, of course, an on-going process. It would be terrific if some of you who see things differently would be kind enough to share your thoughts with me.

It was both comforting and shocking to discover that over a hundred years ago Helmholtz was concerned about ignorance among educated musicians. Comforting in finding that I had an historic ally. And shocking that the same ignorance has continued through the twentieth century.

So what do we do? Let inertia rule? Not rock the music-edu–cation monolith? Toss this writer into the ivory tower with Helmholtz and ignore the "truth" for another hundred years?

Maybe the problem is with book publishers who won't take a chance on ideas that are not mainstream. I think there must be many music educators out there who know many of these "truths" and haven't found an avenue to share their thinking with the rest of us. I'm wondering now, after all of this, whether I should have looked up my music teachers and discussed some of these matters with them before I started shooting off my computer. Maybe they knew more than I thought they did.

I *do* know that my mother and dad knew a lot more about things than they let on when I was a kid. I'm sure they were just trying to protect me until I was mature enough to deal with the "real world." I would like to think that my music teachers, too, were just trying to make things easier for me when they made up cute little things like the "every good boy" stuff.

But, I'm not sure it's always a good idea to make up cute stuff for kids. Sometimes I wonder if the Easter Bunny and Santa Claus are more for the grownups than the kids. It really feels good to give your kids things and pretend that someone else did it. Maybe *that's* what we ought to be teaching them--the joy of anonymous giving--instead of conditioning them to expect to get.

I think kids *can* be told the truth about things. They are more resilient and tough than we give them credit for. As a matter of fact, that's how we *get* tough. When we are confronted with real life, we might actually learn how to deal with it. Hot-housed little flowers simply don't last very long when exposed to a challenging environment. Telling music theory students, "Don't write parallel fifths," without telling them why, doesn't prepare them for the real world of musical composition.

The argument that our music teachers were trying to simplify musical ideas for us just doesn't wash. What could possibly be simpler than supplying experiences of "two-ness" and "three-ness" and letting us *feel* the difference? What is so hard about hearing two pitches *in tune* and comparing them to two pitches *out of tune*? It is a well known fact that languages are easier to learn when we are young. I suspect that musical experiences also can be absorbed more readily when they are provided *before* a youngster is infected with the notion that "learning music is a hard job."

Do you think there is *any* possibility that some teachers pass along to students "rules" that they themselves don't fully under–stand? Hmmmm.....I wonder... Do you think that teachers who don't quite know how music really works tend to unconsciously pass on the impression that learning music is "somewhat mysterious."?

Well, in any case, kids deserve an *honest* education. It isn't fair to fill their heads full of fairy tales and half truths, and then let them grow up and sort out for themselves the real from the fantasy. Those music teachers who *do* know musical truth will simply have to take the trouble to find effective ways of com–municating it to those who don't. Those teachers who don't quite have it together simply MUST improve their own basic concepts or get out of the music teaching business. Poor music teaching is worse, I think, than no music teaching.

At a recent MACCC convention I heard a statistic that really shines a bright light on reality. It seems that a large majority of musicians in "the music industry" are *not* formally trained in music. (I would think that the majority of accountants and lawyers in the music industry are certainly formally trained in their fields.) Could it be that young musicians somehow realize that many, if not most, music teachers are not really "hip" when it comes to the basic principle of the SOUNDS OF MUSIC? Oh, they know that music teachers know a lot *about* music--about music history, about traditional music theory, about musical stylistic practice, about *do-re-mi*'s and about quarter notes and half notes. But they probably also know that a great many music teachers *don't* know how a human hears and organizes musical sounds. THAT is where a musical education should start. And THAT is what has been missing from today's musical institutions of learning.

So, teachers, let's begin telling music students the real truth. We can start by showing them *how music works* instead of stuffing their minds full of artificial constructs and disconnected notational rules. In order to do that, we'll need to re-focus music education toward the *simple basics* of musical sound and perception, so that all those people who have been convinced that they "can't carry a tune in a basket" can discover how a tune is *really* carried--in a mind, heart and "ear" that is in tune with the simple truths of nature.

POSTLUDE

Of course, it's easy to criticize and find fault. I realize that. So I don't want to leave you quite yet without telling you about some of the positive things we're doing to help correct the problems I have been so eager to describe in the preceding pages.

The most important effort is the publication of a new book-- "The Sounds Of Music: Perception And Notation"--that presents the ideas expressed above in a systematic format and assumes no prior musical training. "Sounds" begins by describing in plain language how music works *without* reference to notation, and thereby avoids the traditional pitfalls and common misconceptions described in "Lies." After sound concepts are presented and tied together in a logical and practical manner, music notation is then discussed, showing both its logical and not-so-logical aspects.

A program of sound drills entitled "Natural Ear Training" has also been developed in which the basic elements of the major/minor system are represented in a series of charts. It includes carefully ordered exercises designed to help organize sound experiences. Its most important contribution is that it encourages the development of skills in *acoustic* pitch relations rather than resorting to a keyboard for sound models.

We have received much reinforcement and encouragement from readers of "Lies" and "Sounds" who believe these ideas are sorely needed in music education. However, even music educators who would like to incorporate these practical concepts in their teaching are finding it difficult to do. Since nearly all traditional methods begin with notation and ear-training books invariably begin with scales, it is somewhat difficult to "incorporate" the concepts from "Lies" and "Sounds" into previously used methods. In most colleges, music theory and ear training is a departmental matter, and to get all concerned to abandon comfortable methods used for decades (regardless of moral convictions) is not very probable.

Nevertheless, to assist those hardy souls who are ready for change, we are developing a teacher manual and a student handbook to make the transition easier. Since, I and others have been using "Sounds" and "Natural" in the classroom for a number of years, considerable teaching tips and classroom materials have been developed, so we will be sharing these with any who would like to use them. Publication is expected by the Fall of 2000.

On another topic, Stage 3 Publishing has planned a short treatise on "Components Of Vocal Blend." (Oh, that's right! You already know about this one, don't you.) However, the urgent need for ancillary products to support "Sounds" and "Natural," has delayed "Blend" to a future publication date. When this book finally becomes a reality, it will describe the techniques we found helpful in creating the vocal blend of the L.A. Jazz Choir as well as the choral sounds of many other groups I have been privileged to conduct. If you are into vocal music, I think you will find it practical and effective in unifying the sound of your choral singers. If you're not into producing vocal music, perhaps you may want to give it to a choir director whose group gives evidence that he needs the information. (Just kidding!) Anyway, we'll keep you posted on our web site regarding the publication date.

Are you beginning to think this is sounding a lot like a commercial? Yeah, I guess it does... Oh, well!... In that case, I might as well tell you about some L.A. Jazz Choir recordings you might enjoy. See page 175 for the whats, wheres and hows.

And finally, if you enjoyed reading this book, found it helpful, and would like to inflict it on others, we have included an order form for your convenience. It's on page 176.

Thanks for reading. Keep in touch.

Here's what they are saying about...

THE SOUNDS OF MUSIC: PERCEPTION AND NOTATION

Jerry D. Luedders—Music Chair
California State University, Northridge

"...an exciting new approach to teaching and learning music. One experiences a musical concept which is then supported by listening examples, and lastly by uncharacteristically logical explanations. Eskelin's approach has the capacity to revolutionize the way music fundamentals are taught. It is a book that has been long needed."

Dr. Patrice D. Madura—Assistant Professor of Music Education, University of Southern California

"Enlightening, provocative, analytical and thorough, yet practical and honest. A unique and necessary book for the "sound" learning of music fundamentals. Dr. Eskelin provides a scholarly basis for perceptual understanding through exquisite aural examples, visual aids, and descriptive text; followed by a natural approach to notation learning. A must for music educators."

Paul MacDonald, New Hope International Review, 11/13 /98

The title of this book is a little daunting and, before I opened it, I was expecting an arid, technical work of interest only to serious students of music. This is not the case. The book addresses itself to anyone who wants to develop their understanding of this medium and assumes no prior knowledge. It begins with a laudably succinct chapter on world music which discusses musical traditions and variation. It then goes on to deal with musical concepts such as *timbre*, *tone* and *pitch*. Discussion of the various modes and structure of music follow, including introductions to *melody*, *rhythm* and *meter*. The narrative – which is fluent and engaging throughout – is linked to a CD full of examples to illustrate points made in the text. The book is remarkably user-friendly and, with its A4 format and margin notes, reminded me of the way the *Open University* present their course material. It took me just under a month to work my way through it but I'm glad I took the time. I can now pontificate with some authority about the technicalities of a medium I've always wanted to know more about (but was afraid to ask!). There's bound to be a market for this impressive achievement.

See p. 176 for further information.

NATURAL EAR TRAINING

For developing basic concepts of
- Pitch relations
- Acoustic tuning
- Harmonic structures
- Chord connections
- Melodic principles

The value of a natural approach to ear training is immediately evident to anyone who realizes that keyboards cannot accurately reproduce pitch relations in the same way that ears hear them. While the keyboard is limited to one tuning per digital, the sensitive musical ear naturally tends to adjust tuning according to the harmonic and melodic context of pitches. It follows then that any approach to developing musical aural skills should focus on the nature of relative pitch perception and avoid the compromised sound models produced on a keyboard.

Our current fascination with digital electronics and computerized methods of teaching tends to distract us from natural perception of pitch relations. Unfortunately, accurate acoustic tuning cannot be expressed in digital tuning based on 100 cents (divisions) per "half step." The human ear—even of a novice— is more sensitive than that. Just a single click of the knob can go right past the point of an "in tune" perception. Therefore, it seems unlikely that presently available computer-based drills will lead to success in learning to hear and produce well-tuned pitch relations.

Fortunately, computers and digital drills are not essential to accomplish the task. Youngsters reared in musical environments usually have no difficulty assimilating acoustic truth. For the adult who missed that opportunity, the materials contained in "Natural Ear Training" can help. A simple sustained sound source and a willing and curious spirit can lead to the discovery of harmonic reality and musical insight.

YOUR SATISFACTION IS GUARANTEED!
If you choose to return this item *for any reason*
within thirty days, you will receive a full refund.

TEACHERS
If you adopt Natural Ear Training for your class
and your school orders fifteen or more sets,
the cost of your set will be refunded.

See p. 176 for more information.

L.A. JAZZ CHOIR RECORDINGS

From All Sides

This album was nominated for a Grammy when released in 1986. It contains a variety of music, including jazz standards, a little bebop, a lot of originals and an *a cappella* setting of Miles Davis's *Blue In Green* with soloist Vicki McClure, who moved the world with "Reach Out And Touch" at the 1984 Olympics. The album was recently re-released by Jazz Alliance.

Audio Cassette - $6.50   **Compact Disk - $9.50**

Rosemary Clooney
with the L.A. Jazz Choir
Sings Rodgers, Hart & Hammerstein

Concord Records released this delightful album in 1990. LAJC joins Ms. Clooney on six cuts, including a great John Oddo arrangement of *Oh, What A Beautiful Morning*, (which the group has used as its show opener ever since).

Compact Disk - $9.50

Sweet Dreams
L.A. Jazz Choir with the
Mark Davidson Trio

This album has not been commercially released, and is only available at this time in a pre-release cassette form. But once you hear the great vocal arrangements Davidson did for the group on these six popular standards you won't care about a fancy package. With Mark on piano, the trio rounds out with John Pattituci on bass and Chuck Flores on drums.

Audio Cassette - $3.50

"An Evening of Popular Classics"
VIDEO

This 45-minute video is the latest recording of the L.A. Jazz Choir. It was originally done as an "in house" project, but it came out so well that we are making it available to LAJC fans. Although the video color is not consistently up to commercial standards, the direct-to-digital sound recording is superb. None of these selections were previously recorded by the group.

Video Cassette - $12.50

To order: use the form on page 176.

(Tear out or photocopy this page)

Order Form

Please ship the following items:

Qty.

___*The Sounds Of Music*, w/cd ($37.50)   _____.____
    ISBN 1-886209-13-8

___*Natural Ear Training* ($12.95)   _____.____
    ISBN 1-886209-18-3

___*Lies My Music Teacher Told Me* ($14.95)   _____.____
    ISBN 1-886209-11-4

___*From All Sides* - cassette ($6.50)   _____.____

___*From All Sides* - CD ($9.50)   _____.____

___R. Clooney with LAJC - CD ($9.50)   _____.____

___*Sweet Dreams* - cassette ($3.50)   _____.____

___*Popular Classics* - VHS video ($12.50)   _____.____

                       subtotal _____.____

California orders add 8.25%   _____.____

P&H: $2.50 first item, $1.00 each additional _____.____
    (Option: First class postage, $3.50 per item)

Enclosed check (or money order)   _____.____

Name:_____

Company or School:_____

Address:_____

City:_____ State:____ Zip:_____

Stage 3 Publishing
5759 Wallis Lane
Woodland Hills CA 91367
Website: http://home.earthlink.net/~stg3music/
(Bookstores: please inquire regarding wholesale orders. 818/704-8657)